Psychology of Death & Dying

John C. Morgan
Richard L. Morgan

Wipf & Stock
PUBLISHERS
Eugene, Oregon

For permission to reprint passages on the pages indicated, grateful acknowledgment is made to the following:

Page 4: From *How Could I Not Be Among You?* by Ted Rosenthal (New York: Avon, 1975), pp. 88–89. Reprinted by permission of Persea Books.

Page 9: From *A Death in the Family* by James Agee. Copyright © 1957 by the James Agee Trust. Used by permission of Grosset and Dunlap, Inc.

Pages 12–13: Reprinted by permission of Laura Boone.

Page 70: From *Life after Life* by Raymond Moody (Covington, Ga: Mockingbird Books, 1976). Reprinted by permission of Raymond Moody.

Wipf and Stock Publishers
199 W 8th Ave, Suite 3
Eugene, OR 97401

Psychology of Death & Dying
By Morgan, John C. and Morgan, Richard L.
Copyright©1977 by Morgan, John C. and Morgan, Richard L.
ISBN: 1-59752-405-0
Publication date 10/1/2005
Previously published by Westinghouse Learning Press, 1977

Contents

When It Comes Time to Die
  By John C. Morgan

This morning I fed some sparrows gifts of seed,
remembering one man said God cared for them.
I don't know. I've seen too many creatures fall
to the ground and stay there, still and prayer-less.
But I'll be generous and cast seeds anyway,
just like the Power that made us all.
(Didn't He take pity on another begging soul
who said even dogs get crumbs from the Master's table?)

On bended knee I stay quietly in my garden.
A minute passes. Then one by apprehensive one,
like beggars all, these tiny creatures land--
then skip across the silver ground to feed.
I watch and wait--no panic, no plans.
(Interference only comes when chaos comes).

I watch in wonder this little choir
in boisterous song.
Such joy they have, such Pentecostal fever,
that my ears will burst
or my feet start moving
or my heart shouting!
If I acted like this in church
they'd have the ushers lead me out,
(hushing all the way down tasteful aisles).

My neighbor says we know more loss than gain,
lose a little every day, are stretched taunt by grief,
which is why she has so many wrinkles.
Who am I to argue? She speaks from eighty years
of losing everyone she loved.
She speaks with authority, I with foreboding.

I know I cannot save them all.
But I can still scatter seeds in hope that one or two survive.
And if I make light the burdens of their beating, hungry hearts,
in heaven's eye, that may be enough.
Perhaps He will offer me a few unbroken seeds, so
I can soar on wintry winds when it comes time to die.

Psychology of
Death & Dying

Notes to the Reader

The issues explored in this book are of tremendous significance to us on the threshold of the twenty-first century, both for our increased personal awareness and for the cultural climate in which we exist. Some may argue that we find this world hostile enough to our well-being without contemplating death. In answer it must be pointed out that no one is secure who avoids problems; our deepest meanings are found in looking steadfastly at life in its totality, not in accepting easy illusions.

Death and dying may, at first appearance, seem to be morbid topics, even terrifying topics for some. Consideration of death may arouse unwanted, difficult feelings. Yet we should take comfort from the wisdom of those who have attempted to understand the meaning of death; there is no terror nor final despair in those who have accepted death. Indeed, we may learn how to live deeper lives through exploring the importance of death. To know that we are not gods may provide us with the opportunity to value whatever time we have to live, and to offer thanks for the moments in which we are truly all that we might be.

There will always remain a fear of the unknown; and after all the research, death is still an unknown quantity. Yet it is also the final frontier of human experience. Unless we are open to the creative possibilities of understanding death and dying, there is always the possibility we may remain creatures afraid of living and terrified of our certain end.

John C. Morgan

Introduction

Let us suppose for one moment that you are dying. What can you expect? Doctors, whose role is to sustain life, would rather not participate in your demise. Nurses may suddenly find it uncomfortable to be in your presence. Your family may at first deny your death, and then somewhat resent you for leaving them behind to face loneliness, troublesome finances, and the agonizing ritual of a funeral. In your death, they see their own end.

If you die, you fail. In spite of the inevitability of death, those who surround you at your final moment see no victory in your life's end, but only finality. A terminally ill patient, thinking back over her experiences with doctors and nurses in the hospital, said jokingly that she would like to write a book entitled *Pardon Me for Dying*. Her point was that in facing death with others—co-workers, hospital personnel, clergy—she often felt as if she had to apologize for dying, as if her death were a kind of personal and cultural failure. In fact, various studies have shown that, in institutions, those in the helping professions unconsciously convey to their patients that there is an "acceptable death." The acceptable death is one in which the dying patient expresses no complaints, in which failure is minimized.

Your final moment of life bears little resemblance to the death scenes of romantic literature in which, surrounded by friends and disciples, you utter a few final words of wisdom wrested from life itself. In all probability you do not die at home, but in some institutional setting. If, by chance, a member of the clergy is present at your end, you may expect to hear the traditional phrases that are supposed to prepare you for eternity. (You may feel angry at God.) And if you are among the "elect," your death may be plotted on charts and graphs by researchers studying the stages of dying among terminally ill patients.

No amount of reading or field experience can help you understand death and dying unless you have first confronted your own finiteness—your own death. Each of us has constructed an internal series of mechanisms to deny death its ultimate victory. From our first screaming intake of air at birth, our lives are programmed to deny death, the final obliteration of our personal existence. Yet there is no more deeply personal life experience than death. In the face of such a universal truth, the paradox of death is our denial of its hold on our lives.

Few individuals have explored the state of death and the process of dying as thoroughly as Elisabeth Kubler-Ross, a psychiatrist, who has said, "Death is viewed as taboo, discussion of it is regarded as morbid, and children are excluded from being near the dead and dying with the presumption and pretext that it would be too much for them."*

In the Western world, however, we are probably more death-oriented today than we have been since the days of the Black Plague in the fourteenth century. Yet we still continue to treat death as a forbidden subject.

---

*Elisabeth Kubler-Ross, *On Death and Dying* (New York: Macmillan, 1970), p.6.

Robert Lifton and Eric Olson state, "People have been dying ever since the beginning of time, and yet we know so little about it. People have been dying ever since the world began, and yet each one of us clings to the illusion that death is something that happens to other people, not us."*

---

*Robert J. Lifton and Eric Olson, *Living and Dying* (New York: Bantam Books, 1974), p.8.

1 The Face in the Mirror: Death and the Individual

Objectives

1. To describe the existentialist approach to death and dying

2. To define the concepts of death as described by Martin Heidegger and Miguel de Unamuno

3. To list and describe Kastenbaum and Aisenberg's five general propositions on death

4. To define and describe two death concepts at the individual level

5. To list and describe seven reasons for the fear of death

6. To fill out a questionnaire exploring the significance of the phrase "I will die" and participate in a group discussion of the results

7. To record feelings associated with the death of a significant other person and share these feelings in a group

Accepting Death

Many books on death and dying are theoretical and general. Others are statistical and empirical. But death is intensely personal. It is your "I" which shall perish; it is that uniquely personal dimension of your existence which is to end finally. In many respects, literature, philosophy, and religion provide a deeper insight into the personal dimensions of dying than do statistical studies and field research. Philosophy, it has been said, originates from the fear of death. Buddha knew full well how the fear of death strikes terror in human existence. The Old Testament story of Adam and Eve describes the fall from grace and innocence as a fall into death and freedom.

In a biblical sense, human beings were created "innocent" and had no fear of death until they began to desire knowledge. Original sin and the fall of man is a double-edged sword: persons knowing freedom have choices, but all choices must eventually lead to death. Being free implies making choices until the final act, death, over which there is no decision. Human knowledge and experience make individuality possible, but death puts an end to individuality.

At the age of thirty, Ted Rosenthal, an American poet, is told he has acute leukemia and is going to die. What transpires in the last months of his life provides an intense portrait of the "I" facing death. Rosenthal describes his feelings: "There's something about dying that separates you from all other people. Nobody can come to terms with death. Nobody can walk into death and walk back out the same person."[1]

In a moving conclusion to his life, this poet sums up the personal dimension of death and dying:

But, first, that's alright, go ahead and cry.
Cry, cry, cry your heart out.
It's love. It's your only path.
O people, I am sorry.
Nothing can be hid.
It's a circle in the round.
It's group theater,
No wings, no backstage, no leading act.
O, I am weeping, but it's stage center for all of
   us . . .
Keep moving people. How could I not be among
   you?[2]

It is important to understand that death and dying are not merely to be associated with terminal illnesses, hospital rooms, and funeral homes, the obvious symbols of termination. In a more common way, death and dying begin with birth and take place while we yet live. Every life experience that requires us to let go of a close and intimate relationship—a divorce, loss of friends, departure from familiar surroundings—is a small death, a rupture that touches the roots of our being. Seen in this light, death and dying are the final stage of a process that takes place throughout life.

The Existentialist View of Death

Clinical studies point out the way in which persons die, but literature and philosophy have described death and dying more intensely. Rather than compiling data, an existentialist examines death and dying as a fact of existence. The personal values of the person who is dying are paramount. Although existentialist literature is varied, running the gamut of philosophy from the humanistic agnosticism of Albert Camus to the Christianity of Søren Kierkegaard, it is possible to state a number of general characteristics of the existential approach to death and dying.

1. The existentialist does not see death merely as a rational, objective truth. That death is the biological end of life cannot be denied, but death is intensely personal and involves the mystery of personhood.

2. Death is more than the demise of a thing, the end of an assortment of functions and reactions, the termination of a machine. The whole personal dimension of existence—what makes each of us uniquely human—is tragically bound up with the knowledge that it all must end.

3. Death is not merely an objective truth that can be statistically and empirically monitored and packaged. Death is an ultimate, personal truth involving the whole person. It is not enough to *know* that one must die; one must be grasped by the truth of death in a decisively authentic manner.

4. To the existentialist, death is fundamentally ambiguous. The entire human experience is filled with contradictions and tensions, and death is the primary symbol of this ambiguity. The individual is finite; yet, in moments, the individual can rise above his or her limitations. Each life is moving through time toward death and yet has a strange kinship with eternity because persons can move out of the present and see its relation to the past and future.

Two philosophers, Martin Heidegger and Miguel de Unamuno—both generally grouped into the school of thought known as existentialism—provide an insight into the existentialist interpretation of death and dying.

Heidegger believes the fundamental characteristic of human existence is "care" (*sorge*). By this he understands that we find our being in advance of itself; that is, we are thrown into life before we have found out what it means to exist. Being predates our individuality; life is more than personal existence.

When the individual recognizes his or her own end, life takes on a new, more urgent meaning. Death is the completion of existence; the capacity to anticipate death, to see it within the context of all life, is the basis for understanding human life. Heidegger is not talking about death in general; where death is concerned, each person is alone.

Heidegger gives an *ontological* view of death; it is the final end of all being. Man is *dasein*–beingness. Death is the final form of being-no-more and thus poses the final question of existence. Individuals may run from death, some by throwing themselves into the preoccupations of daily life; this retreat, Heidegger feels, is not authentic. By superficial attempts to avoid death, man estranges himself from the ground of his being. In an effort to run from death, the individual betrays the fact that he is terrified of life.

To Heidegger, death teaches that the extreme potentiality of existence is renunciation, which may occur at any time during one's life span. The authentic person understands his own finitude and understands death as the ultimate confrontation with nothingness. Man comes to understand himself only when he understands freedom grounded in nothingness.

Another early existential thinker, Spanish writer and philosopher Miguel de Unamuno, developed an entire philosophy of death. In his classic work, *The Tragic Sense of Life,* Unamuno recorded one of the most uniquely personal—yet universal—treatises on death ever written. Unamuno writes:

> If I die, nothing has any meaning any more. There are three possible solutions: (a) that I know for certain that I have to die altogether, and then the despair is incurable; (b) that I know I shall not die altogether, and then it is resignation; (c) that I cannot know either way, and then it means resignation within the despair, or despair within resignation, a desperate resignation or a resigned despair, and—struggle.[3]

Unamuno saw the tragic dimension of death in human existence. We yearn to be immortal, to continue ourselves through our children, through our vocations, and —if we are religious—past death itself. And yet reason tells us we must die. The hunger for personal immortality and the fear of death Unamuno believed to be the primal force behind all human endeavors. And this dimension is the tragedy of living.

The rational philosopher David Hume, Unamuno says, was right in concluding that the immortality of the soul cannot be demonstrated scientifically. Rationally, individual consciousness can be shown to end with the organism on which it depends. And yet, Unamuno asks, is there a limit to reason? And how is the individual to survive emotionally, knowing his end is certain and bleak? In the end, Unamuno offers no final solution, but only his hope that human life can be filled with its complete potentiality by living between life and death—affirming neither reason nor faith.

Unamuno believed that there is always a "self of tomorrow," which guarantees the individual that the final self, "the one in death," is the total self in all of its aspects. He said:

> To live is to be dying and to be born again. The person that I am today, my self today, buries my self of yesterday, just as my self of tomorrow will bury today's self. The soul is a cemetery wherein lie all our selves that desisted, all those that we were. But we are left with the consolation of dreaming that when our final self arrives, the one in death, all those that we were, angels of our infancy and youth, will hasten to come round our bed to console us in our last solitude.[4]

A Psychological View of Death

One might argue that the existentialists are wrong in their assumption that death is a primal factor in human experience. The "common sense" approach, after all, is that thoughts of death are "morbid," and so one should think of the passing moments of life, not of its termination. One might ask, for example, exactly what is meant by "living" and "dying." In studying plants and animals, a biologist observes some cases in which it is difficult to distinguish between organic and inorganic material. If we call a body alive because it shows activity, organization, and a more or less stable form in spite of changes, then what is death? While this question may appear somewhat academic, it is an issue that has profound implications. For example, in a hospital setting, at what point is a patient considered "dead"? Often patients are kept alive through artificial means long beyond the time when natural death would have taken place. What exactly is death?

In their classic work on the psychology of death, Robert Kastenbaum and Ruth Aisenberg remark: "We are struck by how little our own field, psychology, has contributed to the understanding of death."[5] They then make five general propositions about death:

1.   The concept of death is relative.

2.   The concept of death is complex.

3.   The concept of death changes.

4.   The concept of death is situational.

5.   The concept of death is related to behavior.

To the individual, there are two basic death concepts. The first is *you are dead*. In this level of awareness, the individual experiences separation from another, knows absence, and senses abandonment. In spite of the terror of the "I" dying that has been described, Arnold Toynbee, the historian, admitted it was the death of a significant other that deeply troubled him. In writing on death and noting particularly his fear of abandonment and isolation if his wife died first, Toynbee said: "There are two parties to the suffering that death inflicts; and, in the apportionment of this suffering, the survivor takes the brunt."[6] For those in helping professions, this truth is important to remember: that even while you deal with the dying person, there is a network of grief surrounding that person—the family and friends.

The second death concept, the one described more frequently by existentialist philosophers, is *I will die*. There is, of course, the "real fear" of impending death among terminally ill patients who have some idea of how long they have to live. There is also the anticipatory fear of death that affects most of us—we know we will die but do not know the month or year. In some cases, not knowing the limits of life may be more terrible because the unknown is always more terrifying.

At the level of individual death, Kastenbaum and Aisenberg note various statements persons ascribe to death: I am an individual. My death is a certainty. My death will occur in the future. I do not know when. Death is a final event. Death is an ultimate separation.

Psychologist Maria Nagy, in studying the attitudes on death among more than three hundred children in Hungary, found what appeared to be three individual phases in attitudes toward death. In the first stage, until the age of five, the child does not recognize death as final. Death is "sleeping." In stage two, for the child from ages five until nine, death becomes personified. There is a "death-man" who takes life away. In the third stage, from nine until ten years of age, awareness strikes the child that death is final and inevitable, like the withering of flowers.

Why is there a fear of individual death? If fear is the response and death the stimulus, the most often repeated reasons for this fear are (a) uncertainty about what comes after death, (b) the event of dying and the pain associated with death, and (c) dread of ceasing to be. Kastenbaum and Aisenberg summarize seven reasons why individuals fear death. There is a fear of

1.   the end of all experiences

2.   life after death

3.   what might happen to the body after death

4.   no longer being able to care for dependents

5.   the grief that one's death will bring to loved ones

6.   the fact that all one's plans will end

7.   a painful death

In an objective way, of course, death is simply cessation of bodily functions. If human beings were objects or machines, death would be less complicated. But, as the existentialists note, we are not simply machines, but persons—and death is the destruction of our personhood. This is not to say that all individuals see death as a terrible enemy. Some view death as the gentle comforter; for those in intense pain, death may come as a relief.

Jose Ferrater Mora, a Spanish philosopher and existentialist, believes that a man is more than his body; he has a mind, reason, and spirit. In his terms, "Man does not have a body, but is his body—his own body. . . . Man is a way of being a body."[7] Because we possess our own bodies, our own beingness, the threat of nonbeing is more terrible personally; it implies that there are forces beyond our control that lay claim to our very existence. Because of our sense of self-importance, every individual movement is a forward thrust toward life, toward the accumulation of living things. And death is the loss of that self-motion, the final, not-of-our-own-making obliteration of personhood.

As mentioned before, literature captures the intensely personal dimension of death more realistically in many respects than the social sciences. It is one thing to study death and dying; it is a far more difficult thing to experience the death of a loved one or to realize deeply and authentically that "I" will die.

In his Pulitzer prize-winning novel, *A Death in the Family*, James Agee describes the dimension of death known only to those who have experienced the mystery and the terror of this ultimate human experience. A man has died; his wife, Mary, has for some time retained her composure. She draws solace from knowing that while there is grief, she is living through it, meeting it. And, in the face of this death, Agee describes surely what must be one of the most beautiful descriptions of grief in literature.

> She thought that she had grown up almost overnight. She thought that she had realized all that was in her soul to realize in the event, and when at length the time came to put on her veil, leave the bedroom she had shared with her husband, leave their home, and go down to see him for the first time since his death and to see the long day through, which would cover him out of sight for the duration of this world, she thought that she was firm and ready. . . . The realization came without shape or definability, save as it was focused in the pure physical act of leaving the room, but came with such force, some monstrous piercing weight, in all her heart and soul and mind and body but above all in the womb, where it arrived and dwelt like a cold and prodigious, spreading stone, that she groaned almost inaudibly, almost a mere silent breath, an Ohhhhhhhhhh, and doubled deeply over, hands to her belly, and her knee joints melted.[8]

Exercises

At the end of each unit, you will find two sets of exercises. The first set covers the background and concepts of the unit; answers to these exercises are given at the end of the book. The second set is open-ended, for use by individuals for personal exploration or by groups for discussion or other activities.

The purpose of this unit is to acquaint you with the reality of death and dying, rather than to provide statistical or theoretical information. For this reason, the exercises that follow permit you to explore individually and in groups your own awareness and feelings toward death. Items 1, 2, 3, and 4 are related to awareness of your own death, and item 5, to your feelings about the deaths of others.

Write T (true) or F (false) beside each of these statements about the existentialist approach to death.

1. Death can become simply a "fact of life."

2. The immortality of the soul cannot be demonstrated scientifically.

3. The fundamental characteristic of human existence, according to Heidegger, is "care."

4. Individuals who become preoccupied and refuse to face the reality of death betray the fact that they are terrified of life.

5. For the existentialist, it is enough to know that one must die.

6. The hunger for personal immortality and the fear of death are the primal forces behind all human endeavors, according to Unamuno.

Circle the letter of the phrase that best answers or completes each statement.

7. Of the following, which represents propositions about death according to Kastenbaum and Aisenberg?
   a. concept of death is relative
   b. concept of death is universal
   c. concept of death is complex
   d. a and c

8. On the individual level, the two death concepts are
   a. you will die, I will die
   b. you are dead, I am dead
   c. you are dead, I will die
   d. you will die, I am dead

9. Psychologist Maria Nagy discovered that the second stage in a child's understanding of death is marked by
   a. denial of death
   b. death is final
   c. death is sleeping
   d. death is personified

10. Of the following, which is not a reason listed by Kastenbaum and Aisenberg for fearing death?
   a. the fear of what might happen after death
   b. the fear of a painful death
   c. the fear that plans will end
   d. the fear that one will lose touch with one's family

Turn to the last page of this book to check your answers.

**Open-ended
Exercises**

1.   As honestly and directly as possible, write your answers to each question in a few simple sentences.

   a. How do you feel about your own death?

   b. Do you think about death frequently?

   c. Do you sometimes feel as if you will not die?

   d. Have you ever deliberately stopped yourself from thinking about death?

   e. Can you really think about your own death? If so, what images come to mind?

   f. In what ways do you deny death?

   g. Have you ever wished you could die? Why?

   h. What does the image of a corpse arouse in your mind?

   i. When was the first time you became aware of death through actual experience? How did you feel about it then?

   j. If you had a choice to make, would you rather die first, before someone you deeply loved?

   k. Have your attitudes toward death changed in the past five years? Why?

   l. Would you really want to know when and how you are going to die?

   m. If you could decide, where would you choose to die and how?

2.   Suppose your doctor has informed you that you have only a short time to live. You have decided that before you die, you want to plan your own funeral and write your own obituary for the local newspaper. On one sheet of paper, write your own death notice. Be sure to include your age, cause of death, and significant life details. On a second sheet of paper, write an outline of your funeral service, showing how you would want it to be conducted.

3.   Discuss your answers to questions a-m and your obituary and funeral service with members of a group, either in a classroom or at home.

4.   Plan a visit to a nearby cemetery or funeral home. While there, pay particular attention to your feelings. Later, make a list of those feelings and ask yourself why you had them.

5.   Read carefully the following excerpt from the unpublished journal of a man who is facing death:

   Inside you scream: No, my God, this is not happening to me. But the doctor's forced smile seems to seal your end more than any words of comfort give you hope.

"We seem to have uncovered a little problem here, Jim," he says holding a clipboard. A little problem, he calls it. I have terminal cancer and that nitwit knows I am dying; he just doesn't know how long it will take.

You tell yourself this is not happening; it is happening to someone else, someone who exists in some other hospital room in some other city. They have confused your tests; you have often teased your friends that hospitals are places where patients go to die, not be made well. People thirty-three don't die. Old people sitting in nursing homes die; young men only die brutally in wars. But when you are thirty-three—and a late bloomer at that—you just don't die.

God, I am afraid. They are talking about me. It is my cells which are being eaten away. It is my soul I watch slipping out of my body. I thought there were no atheists in foxholes. But I am in the deepest of foxholes; deep down in the darkness I see nothing.

I have been dying all my life, dying to the past, dying to everything I have loved. First, my mother and father. I mourned. Then the divorce. More dying, separated from what one has created for ten years: a home.

Listen, you cannot imagine what it is like unless you have gone through it. It is not a single death, but dying to everything which exists. When you are aware that you are dying, you know that everything will die with you. You will not see the trees change in the fall. You will not taste food. You will never again hear the voices of your friends. I am dying to everything.

a. Describe how you would react and feel about this person in each of the following roles: (1) doctor, (2) parent, (3) son or daughter, (4) clergyman, (5) friend, (6) caseworker.

b. Would you rather be this person or his child?

c. What is the difference the person points out between death and dying?

The following poem was written by a nineteen-year-old college coed in the final stages of cancer. While in a cancer ward of a hospital she became engaged to a man with cancer. Six months later her fiance died.

Death Is But a Horizon

Laura Boone

Our relationship has been that of a fencing duel. I, fighting with all my heart, all my energy, and with the resources of my mind. You fought lightheartedly—even teasingly. Because you knew in the end that only you could be the victor.

The usual feints
I won, you won
I discovered a new weapon—interest

I found I could be cold and unemotional
    about you
And so defeat you
You found John and so defeated me
And realized my love, teased and tortured him until he died
Times that I thought I would win
Times that I wished you would
But now the battle's over
Relief
The peace of not having to fight ever again
Perhaps I will forget what it is to "be strong"
You see, I knew all along

What do you think Laura Boone is saying about her own death?

Notes

1.   Ted Rosenthal, *How Could I Not Be Among You?* (New York: Avon, 1975), p. 30.

2.   Ibid., pp. 88–89.

3.   Arturo Barea, *Unamuno* (Cambridge: Bowes and Bowes, 1952), p. 28.

4.   Miguel de Unamuno, *Obras Completas* (Madrid: Atrodisco Aquado Vergara, 1958).

5.   Robert Kastenbaum and Ruth Aisenberg, *The Psychology of Death* (New York: Springer, 1972), p. 1.

6.   Arnold Toynbee, ed., *Man's Concern with Death* (New York: McGraw-Hill, 1969), p. 271.

7.   Jose Ferrater Mora, *Being and Death* (Berkeley: University of California Press, 1965), p. 147.

8.   James Agee, *A Death in the Family* (New York: Avon Books, 1957), pp. 229–230.

Additional Reading

Agee, James. *A Death in the Family.* New York: Grosset and Dunlap, 1963. A novel by the author of *Let Us Now Praise Famous Men.*

Feifel, Herman, ed. *The Meaning of Death.* New York: McGraw-Hill, 1959. One of the first books to confront modern man with the reality of death. A collection of nineteen articles covering death from numerous points of view, including art, music, literature, and psychology.

Glaser, Bernard G., and Strauss, Anselm L. *Time for Dying.* Chicago: Aldine, 1968. Writing for those who work with the dying and for social scientists, the authors deal with psychological aspects of death and dying in the family and the temporal process of dying in hospitals.

Green, Betty R., and Irish, Donald P. *Death Education: Preparation for Living.* Cambridge, Mass.: Schenkman Publishers, 1971. Emphasis on the need for death education in the schools.

Ilie, Paul. *Unamuno: An Existentialist View of Self and Society.* Madison: University of Wisconsin Press, 1967. Author believes key to Unamuno's thought lies in a psychology of paradox, in which the heart and the head are in a state of continual tension.

Kastenbaum, Robert, and Aisenberg, Ruth. *The Psychology of Death.* New York: Springer, 1972. Authors provide a comprehensive overview of death from a psychological perspective.

Kubler-Ross, Elisabeth. *Death: The Final Stage of Growth.* Englewood Cliffs, N.J.: Prentice-Hall, 1975. From personal experience with dying patients, the author shows how, through an acceptance of our finiteness, we can grow; death offers us a chance to discover life's true meaning.

Mitford, Jessica. *The American Way of Death.* New York: Simon and Schuster, 1963. Explosive book makes public the manipulation and commercialism of the American funeral industry. Offers suggestions on how to lower cost and raise the dignity of burial.

Mora, Jose Ferrater. *Being and Death.* Berkeley: University of California Press, 1965. Spanish existentialist views death as an authentically philosophical problem, involved with questions of man, nature, and the structure of reality.

Rosenthal, Ted. *How Could I Not Be Among You?* New York: Avon, 1975. Intense description of a poet facing death from acute leukemia.

Shneidman, Edwin S. *Deaths of Man.* New York: Quadrangle, 1973. Collection of essays dealing with two major questions, how to help the human person who is dying, and postvention, i.e., dealing with survivors after the death of a loved one.

Toynbee, Arnold, ed. *Man's Concern with Death.* New York: McGraw-Hill, 1968. Noted historian terms death "un-American" since the status symbols of America tend to repress the reality of death. Eastern and Judeo-Christian traditions of death are explored as well as frontiers of speculation of beyond death.

2 Faces in the Crowd: Death and Culture

Objectives

1. To compare Eastern and Western cultural approaches to the concept of death

2. To define at least three paradoxes in Western culture related to the concept of death and dying

3. To describe Lifton and Olson's psychohistorical approach to death and analyze its implications for contemporary culture

4. To explain the similarities and differences between Freud's and Fromm's interpretations of the "death instinct"

5. To analyze the concepts of denial and heroism in the theories of Ernest Becker

6. To explain the double-bind denial of death

7. To participate in a group experience on facing the reality of one's own death through a fantasy exercise

Cultural Definitions of Death

Concepts of death and dying are based in certain deeply rooted cultural values. While the commonsense view might be that a death is a death—that is, that once your physical body dies it makes no difference in what culture you die—the fact is that cultural values play a significant role in how individuals define their own deaths. Every culture provides a system of behavior patterns surrounding death; some of these systems can provide emotional and communal support, while others deny death even within the system itself.

We have already noted that concepts of death are relative, complex, changing, situational, and related to behavior. Our concepts of death have changed over time, partly because of changes in our world views and cultural values. One need only look back through history to see that death concepts do change. For example, the Egyptians developed a systematic, ritualistic method of dealing with death. The Egyptian *Book of the Dead* prescribed actions to perform after death; through these actions, the threat of death was lessened, and there was a sense of community in dealing with death. By contrast, in the Middle Ages, where there was less ritual connected with death itself, there nevertheless seemed to be a persistent preoccupation with death; all reality seemed colored by certain religious values, not the least of which were the fear of death and the promise of immortality.

While the major focus of this unit is on contemporary Western cultural values associated with death and dying, it is important to recognize that there are notable differences in cultural values toward death in Eastern value systems. While some would hold that Eastern philosophies are basically death-denying and indifferent, the fact is that Buddha himself based his doctrine on the discovery of human suffering and its causes. Buddha demonstrated that the origins of pain exist at birth and end with the frightful prospect of death. Buddha saw human beings as hopelessly clinging to life; only in the face of death do persons see the vanity of their existence. He saw the inescapable decay of everything created (*anitya*).

Buddha identified various causes of human suffering. The first cause is desire, the tendency to grab and seize life as if it will not end. The second cause of suffering is lack of self-control, leading one to become a slave to one's senses. Beyond these, however, the primal cause of suffering is ignorance, not acknowledging the fact that earthly life is short-lived. Nothing expresses this view more dramatically than Buddha's Hog of Ignorance; snout in the ground, it is concerned only with things at hand, heedless of the sky. In his famous sermon at Benares, Buddha said:

> Learn, O monks, that all existence is naught but pain: inasmuch as death, contact with what one does not like, separation from what one likes or the inability to satisfy one's desires, is painful. . . . The origin of this universal pain is the craving to exist.[1]

For Buddha, a human being is a combination of physical and mental forces. What we call death is the total nonfunctioning of the physical body. What, then, of these nonphysical forces upon the death of the body? Buddhism says volition, desire, will, thirst to live continues manifesting itself after death in another form. In Buddhism, however, there is not an unchanging entity called the self or soul; Buddhism sees no clear point of departure from life into death. The difference between life and death is only a thought; there is a continuity between death and birth, just as the newborn baby already contains within himself a person of sixty.

Buddha attempted to free human beings from their attachments to life, and thus free them from death. And yet, at the moment of his own death, Buddha again cautioned his disciples that there is a nothingness at the heart of things. "All compound things are subject to decay. Work out your end with diligence," he said.[2]

Many Western theorists see that contemporary culture, rather than face death directly, has denied death. In a technological society based on progress and the accumulation of material goods, death seems a total failure over which even technology has no control. However, one need only witness the attempt to prolong life artificially and even to freeze bodies until medical science advances, to understand that technology continues to try to push beyond the limits of life itself.

In contemporary Western culture, furthermore, many are insulated from the personal dimensions of death and dying by the very institutions designed to provide support to individuals. Where once families and friends were personally involved in death, now funeral homes handle most of the final task of burying a family member, who is usually referred to as the "deceased loved one." Where there used to be community participation in death ceremonies, now institutions perform the final rites. It has been estimated, for example, that in the United States about 80 percent of all deaths take place in institutions rather than at home. Those who work in the institutions—the doctors and nurses and social workers—are substitute family members.

The attitudes toward death in contemporary Western technological societies are fraught with paradoxes, of which a number are described below.

1.   While contemporary culture appears to design systems that isolate families and friends from the personal dimensions of death by providing death rites in public institutions, never in human history has the awareness of violent death and the possibility of the total death of humankind been so widely communicated. Marshall McLuhan's Global Village, in which mass communications shrink the size of the world, has become a global nightmare in which mass deaths are communicated daily through the visual media.

2.   While contemporary technology seeks ways to conquer death itself, the common faith in technological progress evident at the beginning of the twentieth century seems to be dwindling. No longer does there appear to be an unquestioned faith in the "goodness" of technology, evidenced by the fact that while technology enables the human race to reach the moon, it also provides instruments of total destruction.

3.   While contemporary culture has a scientific bias, and thus tends to doubt the possibility of personal immortality as one response to the finality of death, there appears to be a cultural countermovement at work in which realities beyond the material world are being sought. The obvious symbols of this countermovement are humanistic-psychology approaches, the return to more traditional religious forms, and the whole spectrum of quasi-religious groupings of persons studying Transcendental Meditation, astrology, and the occult. Whether these movements will have lasting value is not the issue; what is of concern is that, for whatever reasons, individuals find the contemporary rational approach to death lacking in force.

There are frequent dilemmas arising from the paradoxes in the cultural attitudes toward death. For example, in 1860, in a letter to his mistress, the Russian exile Nicholas Ogarev described a death scene that illustrated to him the utter absurdity of cultural values toward death. He describes a man who is condemned to be hanged for attempting suicide by cutting his throat. The man's doctor warns the executioners that it will be impossible to hang the man, since his throat will burst open and he will breathe through the aperture. Ogarev describes what happens:

> They did not listen to his advice and hanged the man. The wound in the neck immediately opened and the man came back to life again although he was hanged. It took time to convoke the aldermen to decide the question of what was to be done. At length the aldermen assembled and bound up the neck below the wound until he died. Oh, my Mary, what a crazy society and what a stupid civilization.[3]

There are other thoughtful writers who, in viewing our cultural attitudes toward death and dying, would repeat with Ogarev: "What a crazy society and what a stupid civilization." The Danish writer and religious thinker, Søren Kierkegaard, illustrates the absurdity of life and death in the following parable:

> Imagine somewhere a great and splendid hall where everything is done to produce joy and merriment—but the entrance to this room is a nasty, muddy, horrible stairway and it is impossible to pass without getting disgustingly soiled, and admission is paid by prostituting oneself, and when day dawns the merriment is over and all ends with one's being kicked out again.[4]

The Cultural Denial of Death

Two contemporary books—*Living and Dying,* by Robert Jay Lifton and Eric Olson, and *The Denial of Death,* by Ernest Becker—stand as hallmarks in analyzing the cultural denial of death in Western civilization.

Lifton and Olson begin with the premise that contemporary Western culture has "buried" death the way Victorian culture pushed sexual questions under the nineteenth-century rug. They note that around the turn of the century, sex was more of a problem than death as a cultural and psychological issue. In sexuality, Freud found what he interpreted as the deeper roots of human personality and behavior. But today Lifton and Olson note, "We are most distanced from the reality of human death. We don't talk about it; we try to conceal, deny, and 'bury' it. But—like the repressed sexuality in Freud's day—death does not go away."[5]

Of course, both Lifton and Olson stress that what makes the question of death new in contemporary life is that for the first time mass death—the obliteration of the human species—is possible. More importantly, they note that without a cultural context in which life has continuity and boundaries, any death is made more difficult. And it is precisely this lack of cultural continuity that they feel permeates contemporary society.

Alvin Toffler's *Future Shock* has shown the devastating effects of too much cultural change too quickly; the alienation and rootlessness of modern man is increased because there are few established cultural systems that have not been threatened from within and without. Death has always been an enigma, the unknown; but cultures have supplied systems that supported continuity in life and thus decreased the fear of dying. That stable, ordered continuity is now evaporating.

Lifton and Olson apply a psychohistorical approach to analyzing cultural values and death. What they mean is that all cultures design systems for dealing with death, some by radically denying death and others by affirming death. What is important is that the way in which a culture deals with death provides—or does not provide—supports to the individual facing his or her own termination. We may, the authors feel, be living in a time of *psychohistorical dislocation,* meaning that our cultural symbols and values fail to supply us with inner psychological meaning. The effects of this dislocation are the intensification of death anxiety and the need to deny the reality of death itself. Groups in culture seek *symbolic immortality*—which is to say, a means of affirming life in the face of death, of finding purposes to sustain life.

Human attempts to seek immortality are varied, both individually and collectively. One such mode of seeking immortality in the contemporary world is ideological totalism, in which a system of ideas or beliefs is shared commonly and held with absolute conviction. The more intense the fear of death becomes, the more fervently the value system is defended.

In contemporary culture, the loss of support systems for those facing death takes a terrible toll on human creativity. In seeking to conceal death, individuals are denied the means of coping. As the historian Arnold Toynbee once wrote, death is un-American. The denial of sexuality eventually led to our sometimes perverse fascination with sex, and various forms of pornography arose. Our denial of death may be leading to a new type of "pornography of death" in which violence and death are glorified for their own sake.

Ernest Becker is a cultural anthropologist profoundly influenced by post-Freudian psychology. Before exploring Becker's analysis of how the denial of death rests at the heart of modern culture, it might be best to summarize Freud's concept of the life instinct (Eros) and the death instinct (sometimes called Thanatos, but not by Freud). Freud was despondent over the destructive forces let loose during World War I. From this experience, he reinterpreted his older theory of sexuality to note that both the striving for life and the striving for death are inherent in life. In his book *Beyond the Pleasure Principle*, Freud explores the basis for his death-instinct theory:

> If it is true that once in an inconceivably remote past, and in an unimaginable way, life rose out of inanimate matter, then, in accordance with our hypothesis, an instinct must have at that time come into being, whose aim it was to abolish life once more and to re-establish the inorganic state of things. If in this instinct we recognize the impulse to self-destruction in our hypotheses, then we can regard that impulse as the manifestation of a death instinct which can never be absent in any vital process.[6]

While the whole concept of a death instinct has been under attack, Freud saw it as an opposing force to Eros, the force that binds and integrates life. The death instinct has the function of separating and disintegrating. Each person, then, has within himself these two contrasting forces, and they are in continual battle. Freud himself only tentatively suggested the death instinct, however, and a number of more orthodox analysts simply discount its legitimacy.

One contemporary thinker who attempts to amend Freud's death-instinct theory is Erich Fromm. Fromm accepts the contradiction between Eros and destruction, between the affinity toward life and the affinity toward death, as being the most fundamental paradox of human life. But Fromm does not accept this contradiction as a part of normal biological growth; rather, Fromm feels the life instinct is primary and the death instinct a form of psychopathology. The religious philosopher Alan Watts also held the view that the death instinct is secondary to life. In his Eastern approach, to be released from reincarnation is to be able to die. This notion sounds similiar to the wisdom of the Zen master who wrote: "While living, be a dead man, thoroughly dead; whatever you do, then, as you will, is always good."[7] In other words, in accepting the inevitability of death, you go beyond anxiety over life.

Ernest Becker begins where Freud left off. For some, his thoughts on death represent a major breakthrough in our understanding of human existence, as deeply significant as Freud's original works on Eros. In Becker's view, it is not death itself that is the enemy, but the devastating consequences of our attempts to deny the inevitability of our own mortality. Becker viewed human beings and their cultures as being concerned fundamentally with the basic struggle to perpetuate life, yet doomed to anxiety by a fear of death and a denial of its finality.

Becker begins by ascribing to the view that as human animals we are hopelessly concerned with ourselves. "In man," he writes, "a working level of narcissism is inseparable from self-esteem, from a basic sense of self-worth. We have learned, mostly from Alfred Adler, that what man needs most is to feel secure in his self-esteem."[8]

To have this primary self-esteem, Becker feels, human beings seek heroism of one sort or another. In this heroism they seek to transcend death itself. Heroism is the need each individual has for self-assertion as an object of ultimate worth in the universe. Becker suggests that this heroic need is the central factor of human existence, because it is based on organismic narcissism and the elemental requirement of self-esteem: "Here we introduce directly one of the great rediscoveries of modern thought: that of all things that move man, one of the principal ones is the terror of death."[9] From this view, Becker feels that heroism is first and foremost a reflex of the terror of death.

There are some who feel that thoughts of death are morbid. But Becker believes that the fear of death is present underneath all the appearances of living. And it can be a fear that is more repressed than others because of the ultimate finality of death. This repression is doubly difficult—human beings are caught in the bind of seeking to affirm their self-esteem, their self-worth, yet knowing that death is literally the conqueror of that sense of self-perpetuation.

In one particularly insightful chapter in his book, "Human Character As a Vital Lie," Becker notes that death provides us with a truth we would rather not face and one that is the root of our denial: that we really do not control our lives. All that culture teaches provides us with the occasion to deny this truth. We accumulate possessions and make money to deny that we will one day be nothing. We seek to perfect ourselves in schools, marry and raise children, and wed ourselves to our need for immortality of self—only to discover at the end of it all that there is no final victory. Frederick Perls drew attention to four layers of neurotic behavior; the fourth and most baffling one was the fear-of-death layer. And this layer, Becker says, "is the layer of our true and basic animal anxieties, the terror that we carry around in our secret heart."[10]

How does Becker provide a way out of the wasteland? There is, to begin with, no final way out of the knowledge that we are mortal. As André Malraux wrote, it takes sixty years of incredible suffering to make an individual, and then he is good only for dying. No matter what method of self-knowledge is used, the individual cannot be given what he most inwardly seeks: immortality.

In his conclusion, Becker provides what is, at best, only a tentative solution:

> I think that life seriously means something such as this: that whatever a man does on this planet has to be done in the lived truth of the terror of creation, of the grotesque, of the rumble of the panic underneath everything. Otherwise it is false. . . . How do we know—with Rilke—that our part of the meaning of the universe might not be a rhythm in sorrow? . . . The most that any of us can seem to do is to fashion something—an object or ourselves—and drop it into the confusion, make an offering of it, so to speak, to the life force.[11]

Ernest Becker, unfortunately, did not live long enough to complete his life work. He died in 1975 at the age of forty-nine. Beyond the image of the heroic individual recognizing finitude yet making an offering to the life-force, Becker might also have ascribed to the joyful selflessness of a Saint Francis of Assisi, who even in the face of death did not deny its power but still loved every living particle of the universe. This was also the wisdom offered by the Russian novelist Dostoevsky, who wrote (in *The Brothers Karamazov*) that to understand the final sad mystery of the universe one must love all that has been created.

The Double Bind Denial of Death

Bernard Glaser and Anselm Strauss report a favorite story about death and hospitals. "Once upon a time a patient died and went to heaven, but he was not certain where he was. Puzzled, he asked a nurse who was standing nearby, 'Nurse, am I dead?' The answer she gave him was, 'Have you asked your doctor?'"[12] Even when death is certain and the patient realizes it, doctors and nurses and other helping professionals play little charades. Richard Erickson and Bobbie Haverstay have shown how a double bind exists in communication patterns surrounding the dying patient.[13] A *double bind* is a situation in which a person is faced with contradictory messages. For example, suppose a mother says to her daughter, "Come here, dear," but her voice is hostile and her body language suggests withdrawal. The child faces a double bind.

Many people think it is proper to conceal knowledge of the patient's impending death. Such attempts are usually useless, however, since patients generally know their condition, whether they are told or not. Such nonverbal cues as moving the patient to an isolated room, the withdrawal of visitors, the hushed voices of doctors and nurses, and the avoidance of the word *death* lead the patient not only to realize the true situation but to join in the meaningless pretense.

Erickson and Haverstay point out that on the verbal level, the patient hears "You will live," but a pattern of nonverbal cues declares, "You will die."

Thus, the patient approaches death feeling there is no one who can be trusted. "All the elaborate efforts and goodwill that go into withholding the truth should rather go into revealing the truth."[14] Doctors, nurses, and other staff members should possess the same skills that psychotherapists use when they neither bluntly confront patients with the truth about themselves nor participate in a deception that hides the truth. Just as psychotherapists try to help patients discover the truth about themselves, doctors and other staff members should alleviate this double bind situation in which dying persons find themselves.

Cultural Buffers and Dying

As we have already mentioned, most cultures provide institutional buffers, or systems of behavioral patterns, developed to provide support to individuals confronted with death. For the greater part of human history, persons have died at home, near family and friends. This custom has at least provided persons facing death with a familiar environment in which to die, among familiar faces. While many may choose to die at home, the reality of contemporary culture is that a steadily increasing number of persons die in public institutions, such as hospitals or nursing homes.

The institutions that surround the dying person, however, appear unable or unwilling to provide the emotional support that the dying patient once received from family and friends. In hospital settings, for example, death may be viewed as a contradiction; if the objective of medical science is to promote life, the dying patient can be seen as a "failure." The same process often seems to be at work in long-term nursing home facilities. Because we are oriented toward the prolongation of life, death strikes a negative note.

In many cases, families or individuals facing death may turn to the church for emotional support. The clergy, however, often have not been adequately prepared to counsel persons facing death; few schools of theology teach courses in death and dying, although there appears to be a new interest in such learning.

The evidence seems to point to Becker's being correct in describing a cultural denial of death—it must be admitted, at least, that in contemporary life there are few institutional buffers to provide individual support in the dying process. For this reason a new support movement has arisen in which groups of persons facing terminal illnesses can discuss their common needs and share their feelings. Groups have been formed for doctors, nurses, counselors, and family members as well as for the patients themselves. This movement and the resulting openness regarding death and dying may signify the beginning of new institutional buffers for dying persons.

Exercises

Place E (Eastern) or W (Western) beside each statement to indicate whether the statement reflects Eastern or Western culture.

1. Because we cling so desperately to life, we are terrified of death.
2. There is no clear departure from life into death.
3. Technology attempts to solve the problem of death.
4. The craving to exist is the origin of our fear of death.
5. Contemporary culture has denied death.

Mark each statement T (true) or F (false).

6. Psychology has long been involved in studying the personal and emotional implications of death and dying.

7. Psychohistorical dislocation occurs when changes lead to pervasive institutional upheaval.

8. Sometimes in the face of anxiety over death, individuals and groups oppress each other.

9. For Becker, the terror of death is principally a fear of what follows death.

10. According to Adler, what human beings require the most is a feeling of self-esteem.

Beside each statement write the letter that identifies its author.

a. Becker
b. Freud
c. Fromm
d. Lifton and Olson

11. The death instinct could never be absent in any vital process.

12. Freud went too far in describing the ultimate power of the death instinct.

13. Modern culture denies death the way Victorian culture repressed sexuality.

14. Cultural groups seek cultural immortality to evade the reality of death.

15. Human beings are doomed to anxiety by the fear of death and the denial of its finality.

Turn to the last page of this book to check your answers.

**Open-ended
Exercises**

1.   Each member of the group writes his or her own eulogy. Then each member of the group lies in the middle of the room, with eyes closed, while the eulogy is read. After all members of the group have been eulogized, share your feelings with the group.

2.   Darken the room as much as possible and give one member a wooden kitchen match. Use this match in some way to represent yourself and your existence. First, respond to the match before lighting it. Then light the match and respond as it burns. Finally, respond to it after it has gone out. The procedure is followed until every member of the group has had a turn; members of the group may want to write down their feelings and discuss them after the experience is over.*

3.   Visit a graveyard in your community and write some of the interesting epitaphs you discover; if this is impossible, bring to class a book of epitaphs. What is the purpose of an epitaph? In the space below write your own epitaph.

---

*Adapted from Abe Arkoff, *Psychology and Personal Growth* (Boston: Allyn and Bacon, 1975), p. 327.

Notes

1. Maurice Percheron, *Buddha and Buddhism* (New York: Harper and Brothers, 1964), p. 30.

2. Ibid, p. 37.

3. A. Alvarez, *The Savage God* (New York: Bantam Books, 1973), p. 43.

4. Ibid, p. 114.

5. Robert Jay Lifton and Eric Olson, *Living and Dying* (New York: Bantam Books, 1975), p. 5.

6. Quoted by Erich Fromm, *The Heart of Man* (New York: Harper and Row, 1968), p. 49.

7. Alan Watts, *Psychotherapy: East and West* (New York: Ballantine Books, 1973), p. 135.

8. Ernest Becker, *The Denial of Death* (New York: The Free Press, 1973), p. 3.

9. Ibid, p. 11.

10. Ibid, p. 57.

11. Ibid, p. 285.

12. Bernard Glaser and Anselm Strauss, *The Awareness of Dying* (Chicago: Aldine Press, 1965).

13. Richard C. Erickson and Bobbie J. Haverstay, "The Dying Patient and The Double-Bind Hypothesis," *Omega* 5 (1974): 287–297.

14. Ibid, p. 295.

Additional Reading

Becker, Ernest. *The Denial of Death.* New York: The Free Press, 1973. Author claims that it is not death itself which is the enemy but the consequences of our attempt to deny death. Man is threatened because he realizes he does not control his life, and the only alternative to despair is offerings made to the life-force.

Brown, Norman O. *Life Against Death: The Psychoanalytical Meaning of History.* New York: Vintage, 1959. Thesis is that mankind must be viewed as largely unaware of its own desires, hostile to life, and unconsciously bent on self-destruction.

Choron, Jacques. *Modern Man and Mortality.* New York: Macmillan, 1963. How to cope with an acute awareness of mortality is explored in this book, which also attempts to explain what death means and "does" to the individual.

Freud, Sigmund. *Beyond the Pleasure Principle.* New York: Bantam, 1959. (Originally published in 1920.) Basis for Freud's view of the death instinct is stated in this classic.

Hendlin, David. *Death As a Fact of Life.* New York: W. W. Norton, 1973. Discusses the type of adjustment needed to face death and reorient one's life after a death.

Kapleau, Philip, and Simons, Paterson. *The Wheel of Death.* New York: Harper and Row, 1971. Collection of writings from Zen Buddhism and other Eastern philosophies on death, karma, and rebirth.

Lifton, Robert J., and Olson, Eric. *Living and Dying.* New York: Bantam Books, 1975. Classic work on the way in which death has been repressed in American society and ways in which people try to achieve symbolic immortality. Authors also explain various modes of immortality.

Rank, Otto. *Beyond Psychology.* New York: Dover, 1941. Because of his fear of destruction, man builds up a world and life all his own to feel secure, but must live beyond psychology through rebirth and conversion.

Stenifels, Peter, and Veatch, Robert M. *Death Inside Out.* New York: Harper and Row, 1975. Doctors, ethicians, and social scientists engage in controversy about such issues as patterns of death in modern institutions, funeral customs and rituals, and the death-with-dignity controversy.

Warden, J. William, and Proctor, William. *PDA: Breaking Free of Fear to Live a Better Life Now.* Englewood Cliffs, N.J.: Prentice-Hall, 1976. Authors discuss the importance of personal death awareness (PDA) and stress the role that a healthy PDA plays in living an authentic life in the present.

3 Stages on Death's Way

Objectives

1. To describe the individuality of the dying process

2. To define the three factors of human viability as outlined by Weisman

3. To describe Weisman's denial, middle knowledge, and acceptance levels in the terminally ill patient

4. To define and illustrate Kubler-Ross' five stages of death and dying

5. To explain how the concept of hope persists in the various stages of dying

6. To list and explain Keleman's three stages of death and dying

7. To describe the four contexts of death awareness according to Glaser and Strauss

8. To illustrate Kubler-Ross' stages of death and dying by participating in a role play of how to relate to a terminally ill person

The Process
of Dying

Most of us do not realize that we are already dying. For this reason we are unaware of the dying process; if we do become aware of our own end, we tend to deny its hold on our life—often by throwing ourselves deeper into the routines of existence: making money, concentrating on our personal and vocational goals, and forming human relationships. While this preoccupation with living is a simple requirement for existence, in one sense it can become a numbing process that enables us to deaden ourselves to death itself.

On a larger scale, Robert Lifton and Eric Olson describe what happens to human beings in this age, facing the terror of total destruction of the species. They say that "numbing" is the characteristic psychological problem of our age. To the extent that this process involves a blockage of feeling, it takes on the characteristics of death. Lifton and Olson say the mind cannot absorb experiences that defy inward meaningfulness. Numbing, of course, forestalls the impact of loss, such as the shock that occurs when a loved one is taken.

Those who work with dying patients find that there are various stages involved in the process, although these stages may not be sequential or occur in the same order. We are individuals, after all, and the way in which we die somehow also reflects the way in which we live. While the image of the serene, accepting person near death may provide a more acceptable symbol, it is nonetheless evident that for some persons resignation or anger may be more in tune with their life experiences. Anger is expressed in the words of the poet Dylan Thomas to his father:

> And you, my father, there on the sad height,
> Curse, bless, me now with your fierce tears, I pray.
> Do not go gentle into that good night.
> Rage, rage against the dying of the light.[1]

Nevertheless, some common stages have been observed in the dying process; one must be careful, however, in understanding that these stages are only general categories and that the dying person retains a single individuality. The American poet Ted Rosenthal, resentfully going through various stages as a terminally ill patient, writes the following account of this process:

> All those people who say that you are predictable and that you will die in the same way that everyone else dies, they are right. I resented that at first. I resented them saying 'Oh you are at the two-week stage. You're feeling, doing this. You're free. You're at the angry stage. You're lost. . . . Well, they're right. It works that way with me. I am following patterns. I am following the guidelines for dying-of-terminal-cancer patients down to the letter.[2]

Dr. Avery D. Weisman is a psychiatrist who describes the stages of dying from actual clinical experience at Massachusetts General Hospital. Dr. Weisman, however, believes that the observation of dying patients, no matter how great a number, cannot solely define the dying process. In some cases, he feels the purely scientific model can numb one to the existential reality of death, to the impact of personal extinction. For Dr. Weisman, there is no appropriate death. Rather there is purposeful death—a death that one might choose for oneself if a choice were possible. Death with dignity, after all, means individual choice in concert with the individual's own life values and experiences.

To describe the dying process, Dr. Weisman conducted interviews with over 350 patients during a four-year period. The patients, by and large, were cancer patients, older persons, persons thought to have a terminal illness, or individuals who were preoccupied with death. From the extended interviews, Dr. Weisman noted: "The process of dying takes place in many ways and on different levels of experience. We die to many things before we die of a disease. Small, partial deaths gradually become confluent, so that we may cease to be as an autonomous person long before literal terminus takes place."[3]

The full sense of human viability or "aliveness," Weisman believes, is determined by three factors: biological survival, competent behavior, and responsible conduct. Biological survival means that the dying patient can experience relief from pain and reduced suffering and can adapt to diminished strength. Competent behavior implies that a dying patient can choose the way he or she solves problems and carries out regular tasks. Responsible conduct means self-direction and fulfillment of the patient's own ideals. Each of these is related to significant survival.

Weisman also defines the beginning and ending points in the stages of dying as initial denial and final acceptance.

Weisman sees denial as a dynamic process, most often related to the jeopardized relationship with a significant key person. The function of denial is not simply negative. Denial can also provide a means of coping. It can help to maintain a simplified relationship with significant others.

Somewhere between denial and acceptance, Weisman sees a gray area he calls "middle knowledge." (See Figure 1.) As a rule, he notes, middle knowledge tends to take place at major transition points in the dying process: when patients begin the descent into death, undergo a setback, or notice disruptions in relationships with important persons in their lives. At this stage, the patients appear unpredictable. They want to know about their disease, but they do not want to know. Weisman says the middle-knowledge stage heralds a relapse, usually into the terminal phase.

Figure 1.
Stages of Death and Dying (Weisman)

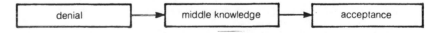

In all cases, the meaning of death must be related to the person dying. How does the dying person look upon suffering? What does death signify to the dying person? Who are the key people? What has mattered most in this person's lifetime?

Weisman would want those dealing with dying patients to remove the wholly negative connotation of death:

> Our death is also part of being alive, and is within reach, although we do not reach out for it. Despite our cultural indoctrination, death is not the essence of corruption and negativity. Human values seem to be enhanced when we become aware that death always surrounds us, like the shadow that illuminates the substance.[4]

The Work of Kubler-Ross

The contemporary thinker and doer who has most profoundly brought to light the deeper meanings of death and dying is Elizabeth Kubler-Ross, whose work among dying patients has essentially taught us that those who know they are dying have a great deal to say about living—another paradox to consider. Kubler-Ross, from direct relationships with terminally ill patients, has outlined various stages in the dying process in terms of patients' coping mechanisms at the time of the terminal illness. (See Figure 2.)

Figure 2.
Stages of Death and Dying
(*Kubler-Ross*)

The first stage Dr. Kubler-Ross calls denial and isolation. It is most frequently represented by this response of the patient who is told of the terminal illness: "No, not me, it can't be true!" Denial is typically an initial response, and it can occur throughout the length of the illness in one form or another. In agreement with Weisman, Kubler-Ross suggests that denial serves the function of providing a buffer between the initial shock of being told one has a terminal illness and one's sense of self-esteem. While denial may last until death, Dr. Kubler-Ross found that in some two hundred terminally ill patients interviewed, only three attempted to deny death to the last. She writes:

> The need for denial exists in every patient at times, at the very beginning of a serious illness more so than toward the end of life. Later on the need comes and goes, and the sensitive and perceptive listener will acknowledge this and allow the patient his defenses without making him aware of the contradictions.[5]

It is later that the patient uses isolation more than denial. Isolation is a form of denial, in some respects, because the patient retreats from the pain that the realization of impending death brings.

"Why me?" represents the second phase of the dying process. This stage is most frequently a time in which it becomes extremely difficult to deal with patients, whose anger is displayed at random.

From the patients' point of view, Kubler-Ross points out, anger is well founded. "Maybe we too would be angry if all our life activities were interrupted so prematurely," she notes.[6]

Having passed denial and anger, the patient enters the third stage, the stage of bargaining. The dying patient wishes only for an extension of life and a release from pain and suffering. To gain such an extension, various bargains are made. "If I really stop smoking, maybe I can live another few months," one patient remarked.

"Bargaining," Dr. Kubler-Ross says, "is really an attempt to postpone; it has to include a prize offered for 'good behavior'; it also sets a self-imposed 'deadline'. . . and it includes an implicit promise that the patient will not ask for more if this one postponement is granted."[7]

In some cases, bargaining is closely allied with some form of guilt. The patient, recognizing that life is dwindling, wishes to make amends for some past failure; in doing so, he or she surmises that life will be extended.

The fourth stage of dying is depression. The patient, who no longer expects to recover, is beyond denial and anger. The loss of life becomes overwhelming. Up to this stage, however, the patient has been considering the loss; there has been preparatory grief, in which the patient prepares for the end.

The first type of depression is therefore self-directed; it anticipates the loss of the individual's world. A second type of depression takes into account impending losses. Depression becomes a means of preparing oneself for the loss of all love objects. This second type of depression tends to be silent, a preparation for the end.

The final stage of dying is acceptance. It is not, as many suppose, a "happy time," but practically void of feelings. Kubler-Ross describes this last phase in these terms:

> If a patient has had enough time . . . and has been given some help in working through the previously described stages, he will reach a stage during which he is neither depressed nor angry about his 'fate.' He will have been able to express his previous feelings, his envy for the living and the healthy, his anger at those who do not have to face their end so soon. He will have mourned the impending loss of so many meaningful people and places, and he will contemplate his coming end with a certain degree of quiet expectation.[8]

Throughout all the various stages of dying, hope persists in some form. This hope is the trust that in spite of the pain and suffering, dying must have a meaning. Conflicts in hope generally arise when those surrounding the patient convey hopelessness at a time when the dying person still needs to hope; conflicts also take place when those surrounding the patient cannot accept the patient's need to die.

Other Views of Dying

Roy Branson has argued that Kubler-Ross' stages are ambiguous and not merely descriptive, but prescriptive. The final stage, acceptance, is normative for Kubler-Ross, but if patients do not follow this script, they run the risk of being considered failures, or of forfeiting the compassion of those who care for them, just as terminal patients who showed signs of despair or withdrawal were considered ungrateful and uncooperative by hospital personnel in the fifties. Branson claims that if patients move from acceptance to another reaction, they are thought to be regressing. Questioning whether the stage of acceptance is natural, Branson states that "acceptance of death returns the dying to a juvenile inability to face the facts; that the infantlike dependency and passivity of Kubler-Ross' stage of acceptance is the greatest sort of denial of death's reality."[9] Branson believes that the doctor or nurse should accept the person, not expect the dying person to accept the unacceptable.

Branson indicates that dying patients do not always follow the script. In some cases, the patient will go through Act 2 of the stages (anger) after going through Act 3 (bargaining), or jumble three or four acts into one big scene. Ivan Illich has claimed that the ultimate intransitive activity—dying—is now being managed by professional thanatologists. "Thanatologists who know what the four or five stages prior to death ought to be now educate you to practice them in the correct sequence."[10] However, Kubler-Ross' studies of dying patients are among the first psychiatric studies to interpret the dying person's "hidden" language and feelings as a precondition for counseling.

Stanley Keleman restructured Kubler-Ross' five stages of death and dying into three stages, divided according to the state of consciousness of the dying person. (See Figure 3.) In the resistance stage the dying employ anger, denial, bargaining, fight, and avoidance. In the review stage a new consciousness is discovered, since the whole of one's life comes in a flash, in a single shot, under very sudden circumstances. "In this stage a lot of pain and struggle disappear as one comes in contact with unfinished business and reowns part of the self, thus developing another type of consciousness, at one with himself, rather than images of the past."[11] In the third stage the unconscious prevails as it does at birth. Persons who have recovered from this stage, such as heart victims rescued through heart massage, talk about dying as a warm ecstasy.

Figure 3.
Stages of Death and Dying
(Keleman)

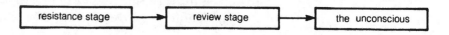

Barney Glaser and Anselm Strauss have devised a theoretical model of "dying awareness" that posits four sets of relationships between the patient and those who provide care.[12] (See Figure 4.)

Figure 4.
Stages of Awareness in Death and Dying (Barney Glaser and Anselm Strauss)

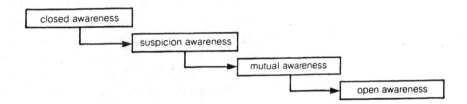

Closed Awareness   This state is described as "keeping the secret." The patients do not know that they will probably die, but family and medical personnel do. The staff thus invents a fictitious future that they believe will help the patients.

Suspicion Awareness   The patients suspect that they are going to die. They get hints, may even get the message. Thus there is a contest for the control of information, with the patients really wanting to have their suspicions disproved.

Mutual Awareness   The third context of awareness is called the "ritual drama of mutual pretense," or "let's-all-pretend." It is a masquerade, as Glaser and Strauss call it, in which all the ingredients of a stage play are present. Masks to hide the real feelings of all concerned; costumes, in which patients dress as if they were not going to die; and stage props in which the hospital is fixed so that it resembles home.

Open Awareness   In the fourth and final stage of awareness, both patient and medical staff openly acknowledge the reality of approaching death. Two inquiries are involved. "Will I die?" and "How and when will I die?" The patient becomes resigned to death, and the family grieves *with* the patient, rather than simply *for* the patient. Open awareness does present a problem. In Robert Neale's words, "How is the patient going to present his dying self to the world?"[13] As a rebel who does his own fighting? As a brave and stoic person who grimly accepts fate? Open awareness asks the patient to find an identity at a time when pain diminishes the person's ability to act and think normally.

For those who deal with dying persons, whether at home or in an institutional setting, a word of caution must be added: there is no "right way" to deal with the individual who is dying. There are clues, however, that one must pay attention to in order to provide an environment in which the dying person retains some measure of authenticity and personhood. "Death with dignity" does not mean that every person accepts death, but rather that a person's death represents a continuation and affirmation of his or her life style. Institutional definitions of death may, for example, run counter to what a person defines as appropriate for his or her own death. A woman who has struggled for fifty years to provide for her family may find it difficult at the end to be restful and accepting. An appropriate death for this person may require defiance and more struggle, and because of her values, this struggle would be "death with dignity." Those who work in institutions where persons are dying should be acutely aware of the individuality of death as well as of its stages.

The descriptions of death and dying by Weisman, Glaser and Strauss, and Kubler-Ross derive from their work with terminally ill patients. From these patients, they say, we can learn something about living. Perhaps the stages of dying correspond to stages of life that those of us who cannot predict our own death must go through. If death is the final separation, what of those other separations in our lives—a divorce, loss of a job, a move to a new community? In a very real sense, any separation from an ultimate concern, to use the phrase of theologian Paul Tillich, is a "small death"—and moving toward this small death, might not each of us travel through the phases of dying? If a significant portion of our lives requires us to let go of meaningful relationships or concerns, then understanding the meaning of the final letting go—of dying—can be of tremendous importance to each of us.

Abraham Maslow faced death when he suffered a severe heart attack; later he described how he learned from this experience to make life more meaningful. In a letter written while he was recuperating, he said,

> The confrontation with death—and the reprieve from it—makes everything look so precious, so sacred, so beautiful, that I feel more strongly than ever the impulse to love it, to embrace it, and to let myself be overwhelmed by it. My river never looked so beautiful. . . . Death and its ever-present possibility makes love, passionate love, more possible. I wonder if we could love passionately, if ecstasy would be possible at all, if we knew we'd never die.[14]

Exercises

Circle the letter of the phrase that best answers or completes each statement.

1. According to Weisman, the sequence in the stages of death and dying is
    a. acceptance, denial, middle knowledge
    b. middle knowledge, denial, acceptance
    c. denial, acceptance, middle knowledge
    d. denial, middle knowledge, acceptance

2. Which of the following statements represents Weisman's views?
    a. There is an appropriate death.
    b. The observation of dying patients defines the dynamic process of death.
    c. A purely scientific model of death and dying is needed.
    d. Death should be purposeful and involve an individual choice.

3. According to Weisman, competent behavior in death means that
    a. the dying patient chooses the way to solve problems and carry out regular tasks
    b. the dying patient has pain relief
    c. the dying patient can fulfill his or her own ideals and self-direction

4. According to Weisman, the function of denial
    a. blocks the patient's awareness of death
    b. is not totally negative, since it provides a means of coping
    c. is related to Kubler-Ross' second stage
    d. none of the above

Before each description write the letter that identifies which of Kubler-Ross' five stages the patient appears to be in.

a. denial and isolation
b. anger
c. bargaining
d. depression
e. acceptance

5. Mrs. K., 41, has asked that she be permitted to return home one more time in order to see her own physician, who once helped her through a serious illness.

6. The young man has been screaming at his fiancée. He tells her that she has not been to see him for some time and is probably already looking for another boyfriend.

7. The older gentleman has not spoken for some time. He refuses to eat and often can be observed staring out of the hospital window.

8. Mrs. H. is somewhat silent. She appears devoid of feelings, but she will answer questions directly. She spends less time talking with her husband but is happy when he holds her hand.

9. James wants to go home. He claims the doctors have not acted wisely or made the correct diagnosis in his case.

Beside each situation, write the letter of the awareness stage that is illustrated.

a. closed awareness
b. suspicion awareness
c. mutual awareness
d. open awareness

10.   Mr. Gould has discovered that he is dying but doesn't admit this to his family.

11.   Nurse Waite is direct and honest in talking to patients about their death.

12.   Mrs. Neely is always asking the nurses about her illness, suspecting she has terminal cancer.

13.   Dr. Hunter decided that he would not inform Mrs. Rowe that she was dying of leukemia.

Turn to the last page of this book to check your answers.

Open-ended Exercises

1.   After a discussion of Kubler-Ross' stages of death and dying, four members of the class role-play a terminally ill patient's experience of these stages. One student plays the patient, another the doctor, a third a nurse who facilitates the patient's expression of feelings at each stage, and the fourth a nurse who blocks the patient's feelings. As the patient moves through the stages of denial and isolation, anger, bargaining, depression, and acceptance, one nurse is an empathic counselor-friend; the other nurse is indifferent.

2.   Fantasize that someone close to you—a friend, a parent, a spouse, a lover—is dying. In the space below write your personal feelings about this loss.

Share your feelings with other members of the group.

Notes

1. Oscar Williams, ed., *Modern Verse* (New York: Washington Square Press, 1963), p. 574.

2. Ted Rosenthal, *How Could I Not Be Among You?* (New York: Avon Books, 1975), pp. 26–27.

3. Avery D. Weisman, *On Death and Denying* (New York: Behavioral Publications, 1972), p. 57.

4. Ibid., p. 225.

5. Elisabeth Kubler-Ross, *On Death and Dying* (New York: Macmillan, 1974), p. 41.

6. Ibid., p. 51

7. Ibid., p. 84.

8. Ibid., p. 112.

9. Roy Branson, "Is Acceptance a Denial of Death? Another Look at Kubler-Ross," *Christian Century* 88 (May 7, 1971), p. 476.

10. Ivan Illich, "Medicine Is a Major Threat to Health," *Psychology Today* 9 (May 1976), p. 74.

11. Stanley Keleman, "Stages of Dying," *Voices* 10 (Summer 1974), p. 47.

12. Barney Glaser and Anselm Strauss, *Awareness of Dying* (Chicago: Aldine, 1965).

13. Robert Neale, *The Art of Dying* (New York: Harper and Row, 1974), p. 19.

14. Quoted in Abe Arkoff, *Psychology and Personal Growth* (Boston: Allyn and Bacon, 1975), p. 324.

Additional Reading

Berman, Eric. *Scapegoat: The Impact of Death-Fear on an American Family.* Ann Arbor: University of Michigan Press, 1973. A naturalistic observation of how seven persons in a family react to death.

Cartwright, Ann; Hockey, Lisbeth; and Anderson, John L. *Life Before Death.* Boston: Routledge and Kegan Paul, 1971. Study of 960 recently deceased persons in England; includes memoirs of the last year of their lives.

Fulton, Robert. *Death and Identity.* New York: John Wiley, 1966. Research into grief attitudes toward death. Death defines man's existence and asks for our identity. Excellent section on grief includes three stages of emancipation from deceased, readjustment to environment, and forming of new relationships.

Glaser, Barney G., and Strauss, Anselm L. *Awareness of Dying.* Chicago: Aldine, 1965. Contexts of awareness in facing death: closed awareness, suspicion awareness, mutual pretense, and open awareness. Helpful to all who work with the terminally ill.

Jung, Carl. *Modern Man in Search of a Soul.* New York: Harcourt, Brace, and World, 1933. Modern man's concern for spiritual realities in later life enables death to lose its terrors and become a meaningful part of the life process.

Kavanaugh, Robert. *Facing Death.* Baltimore, Md.: Penguin Press, 1974. Stages in grieving are explained, from shock to relief to reestablishment.

Kubler-Ross, Elisabeth. *On Death and Dying.* New York: Macmillan, 1970. Studies of dying patients led to analysis of five stages that lead to the acceptance of death. Dying patients have much to teach the living.

———. *Questions and Answers on Death and Dying.* New York: Macmillan, 1974. Basic questions about the dying process, with answers given by Dr. Kubler-Ross. A practical guide for dealing with death-related issues.

Pearson, Leonard. *Death and Dying: Current Issues in the Treatment of a Dying Person.* Cleveland: Case Western Reserve Press, 1969. Collection of articles on dealing with the terminally ill. Excellent one hundred-page bibliography on death and dying.

Weisman, Avery D. *On Dying and Denying: A Psychiatric Study of Terminality.* New York: Behavioral Publications, 1972. A vivid portrayal of the stages of dying described from clinical study, with particular concern for the stage of "middle knowledge" between denial and acceptance.

4 Grief and the Dying Person

Objectives

1. To define three types of grief

2. To describe Kavanaugh's seven stages of grieving

3. To discuss the positive aspects of anticipatory grief, both for the patient and those who must relate to the patient

4. To describe the feelings of family members associated with "sudden death"

5. To determine the ways in which guilt plays an important role in the grieving process

6. To explain the different reactions of children to death and grief

7. To describe three creative ways to ventilate grief according to Edgar Jackson

8. To participate in a group role-playing situation where the expression of grief is facilitated by helping persons

The Process of Mourning

The process of mourning or grieving is essential for personal adaptation to loss. It is necesury whether the loss is a result of death, termination of a relationship, a change in life style, or a change in situation.

Through mourning, one learns to adjust to the changes that must occur following a loss. If the process is unsatisfactory (if one has not completed this process), then the chances of healthy adjustment to the loss are not as great.

There are several types of grief. There is *anticipatory grief,* which is mourning the loss of someone or something before the loss occurs. There is *grief after the death,* which takes place after the occurrence of the loss and can be divided into two types of mourning, the type of grief one experiences after having gone through anticipatory grief and that which occurs when there is no warning of impending loss. The second type is referred to as *sudden death.*

Dr. Robert Kavanaugh, a former priest and teacher, currently a counselor, in his book *Facing Death* devotes one chapter to the process of mourning. This chapter, "Understanding Human Grief," outlines seven stages of grieving: shock, disorganization, volatile emotions, guilt, loss and loneliness, relief, and reestablishment.[1] The stages do not necessarily occur in sequence, and overlapping or duplication may occur; with some understanding of the stages of grief, however, one may have an easier time coping with the mourning process.

Figure 5.
*Stages in the Grief Process
(Robert Kavanaugh)*

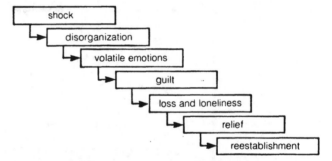

The first stage of grief is *shock,* which is experienced when one learns that someone close has died or is terminally ill. At this stage the mind blocks the reality of what it has learned. To give advice to the mourner at this point is useless because the individual denies reality for protection. The best an outsider can do is be there to listen and sympathize. Erratic behavior can be expected when an extrovert finally realizes that the death or terminal illness is a reality. "Explosions can take place in the form of hysteria, screaming, pounding, or breaking valuable objects."[2] From one who is an introvert, withdrawal as well as escapism can be anticipated.

The griever has an easier time passing to the second stage, *disorganization,* if he or she feels loved and accepted by other important persons. At this stage the bereaved's perceptions of reality are not clear. Persons react inappropriately to situations; their emotions may be out of touch with the rest of the world. The individual engulfed by grief expresses emotions through excessive crying or talking. Kavanaugh points out that because of the emotional intensity of the stage, the mourner has a difficult time making decisions and, therefore, should be encouraged to postpone important decisions until some later date.

The third stage, that of *volatile emotions*, is closely linked to anger in Kubler-Ross' five emotional stages of death and dying. The griever strikes out at God or the deceased or some other convenient love object. This anger, or volatile emotional reaction, stems mainly from helplessness, hurt, and frustration.[3] Unable to cope adequately with these emotions, the individual rebels.

Guilt can block the expression of anger. If this anger is unexpressed, it may result in years of pent-up rage. This unexpressed rage must come out in some form or other and may cause migraine headaches or other physical ailments. All individuals do not express anger or rage in the same manner, however. Some bereaved persons simply retreat into sadness as an expression of anger. It is important that an angry mourner be allowed to vent emotions fully without being judged so that the psyche can begin to heal.

The fourth stage is that of *guilt*. It is during this time that the grief-laden person's conscience begins pricking with regret about things that were done or not done while the deceased was yet alive. The mourner who idealizes the past will feel responsible for failures. Guilt may also result from the belief that one could have prevented the death of the deceased in some way.

At this stage, the bereaved simply needs to hear from someone else that there is no reason to feel guilty. Following such reassurance, guilt may subside. Kavanaugh recommends that the consoling thing to do is to listen and allow the bereaved to forgive himself or herself. The need to be accepted is extremely important.

Loss and loneliness is the fifth stage of grief. The pain that is experienced during this stage is the deepest. The awareness that a person once lived and occupied space becomes overwhelming as reminders enter one's everyday life. The empty bedroom or the unused archery set now becomes a source of pain. The full impact of the person's death becomes a reality to the survivor. Even if the relationship was a poor one, something is missing; a sense of loss prevails.

This stage appears to be dangerous. The empty space that now exists desperately needs to be filled. The griever forgets the faults of the deceased and attributes godlike qualities to the person who is gone. The danger enters in when the bereaved transfers these qualities to someone else. For example, a mother may seek replacement for her husband through her son and burden him with high expectations. Or she may marry on the rebound to fill this gap. And in doing so, she may try to remake the new spouse into the old.

Kavanaugh warns that replacement is impossible. He stresses that "the new love can grow in the same ground as the old, share the same life style and bed, but the roots of any former love are so entwined in the bereaved heart that no new love can uproot or replace them."[4] The bravest thing to do is to face the loss rather than to replace it or busy oneself attempting to repress it. Escapes will prevent mourning, which is necessary to allow recovery. For the bereaved to get on with a new life, complete grieving and complete healing are essential.

The sixth stage, and the next-to-last, is *relief*. As negative as this concept may seem at the time of death, the survivors may sense relief of one form or another. For example, if the deceased experienced a great deal of pain before death, the survivors may be relieved that the person is no longer suffering. And when an individual who needed medical treatment dies, there may be relief that bills will cease to mount.

Another aspect of relief is more complicated. No matter how much an individual loved the deceased, some degree of relief is usually experienced. Kavanaugh claims:

> Few, if any, vibrant relationships when honestly appraised do not coexist with a host of speculations on what it might be like to be free from demands of spouse and children, to taste another style of life, to try another mode of love or sex, to find a still more rewarding answer than the present loves seem to offer. In these similiar fantasies reside the causes of the normal relief most mourners feel at the time of death.[5]

This stage is difficult for the mourner to face because it goes against what is normally considered to be real grief.

Kavanaugh points out that the basis for much of this relief is the constant quest for a more perfect love, one that may be more fulfilling. The bereaved who cannot accept this as normal may feel guilty about realizing such an emotion. It is vital that the griever express relief with the understanding that it is normal.

The seventh and final stage is that of *reestablishment*. This stage develops slowly as the mourner learns to deal with guilt and many dreams are gradually brought into real life. The deepest grieving fades, and the individual begins looking to the future with new hope. Reminders that the deceased once lived become less painful. The desire to become involved with life begins taking hold.

The difficulty at this stage is the fear and guilt the bereaved may experience from a feeling of moving to a new life too quickly. If the belief occurs that others will find this ability to enjoy life disgusting, the growth into reestablishment may be hindered or stunted.

Old friends and new friends are important at this time. Old friends give encouragement for the bereaved to reestablish himself or herself. New friends offer the bereaved an opportunity to be viewed in a new light. The need of the griever to be viewed as an individual, not just as a person in mourning, makes new friends important.

On the other hand, pushing an individual into reestablishment too soon may hinder the process. Parents who have lost a child, for example, should not be persuaded to have another child or to adopt one too soon, because haste may lengthen the grieving time. Reestablishment can be compared to other stages of growth and development: a baby who is taught to walk before crawling may not learn to walk properly. Each person must be allowed enough time to make the changes that are necessary.

G. Gorer discovered three types of behavior among bereaved people who, for one reason or another, were unable to face death, to grieve, and to recuperate. These behaviors are hiding grief by busyness, glorification of the dead person, despair. Kubler-Ross suggests that many widows and widowers who come to their physicians for help are showing "somatic symptoms" as a result of their failure to work through grief and guilt. Gorer also cites a study by Clayton (1971) where more than eight percent of the bereaved experienced crying, depression, and disturbed sleep, while difficulty in concentration, lack of appetite, and reliance on medicines characterized more than half of those in the study.[6]

Anticipatory Grief

Anticipatory grieving occurs before a person dies; it allows an individual to prepare for his or her own death or the death of a loved one. Both the mourner and the terminally ill person may pass through the stages of grief, if both persons acknowledge the terminal illness. Acknowledgment is best handled when the terminality of the loved one is openly discussed. It is important that such discussion take place when the persons involved are prepared to discuss it.

For those involved, it may mean listening for what Kubler-Ross refers to as "symbolic language." One must look and listen for cues indicating that a person is ready to communicate that he or she is dying, whether this communication be verbal or nonverbal. Loved ones of the terminally ill may also relate symbolically when they want to know about someone's terminal illness but are afraid to discuss it directly. Kubler-Ross claims that one of the most common forms of symbolic language is demonstrated when a dying patient talks about another dying patient in the hospital, although the person really wishes to discuss his or her own death. Another form may be taking hold of someone's hand. If the message is misinterpreted, however, and the listener begins forcing a dying person to discuss impending death prematurely, the experience could be traumatic for the individual. If the family and other loved ones are forced to face the death of the terminally ill person before they are prepared, the result may be denial.

Denial of the person's illness while he or she is yet alive is not uncommon, either for the dying person or for the family. Denial may result in seeking the diagnosis of another or several doctors to verify what the persons involved hope is not true. Unfortunately, if it lasts until the person dies, denial makes it difficult for the family to accept the death.

As was mentioned earlier, anticipatory grief allows loved ones to clear up "unfinished business," or matters that have been unspoken for a period of time. A dying mother and her daughter may patch up an old feud, for example. This helps alleviate some of the guilt involved with dying. If loved ones can discuss the impending death of a member of the family, the discussion may allow them or the dying person to take care of financial matters, wills, or funeral arrangements. Such discussions may seem morbid, but many grief-stricken survivors are confused by legal and financial matters regarding death and cannot make rational decisions about them immediately following the death of a loved one.

Another advantage of anticipatory grief lies in the time factor. If death can be anticipated, persons close to the terminally ill are usually better prepared for death and may more easily accept it when it occurs.

Anticipatory grief is prevalent in some relationships because of their very nature. For example, as parents and relatives age, the fact that they will die becomes a reality. As a married couple ages, each person anticipates the death of the spouse and begins to grieve long before the death itself takes place. This anticipation can serve as a cushion for the death.

The negative side of anticipation is the "unfinished business" that has not been resolved and is complicated by additional problems that enter into the relationship because of the terminal illness. The nuclear family system, which involves only parents and their children, holds few buffers within it when a member of the family dies, particularly when an adult member passes on. The responsibility that lies with the dying person must be taken over by other members of the family. For example, a wife may resent the fact that her husband is dying when she realizes that she will soon have to be the breadwinner. A child may resent a parent's death and experience feelings of rejection. These feelings of resentment and guilt make it difficult for the members of the family to accept the death of the dying individual.

Regardless of the negative aspects, it is always easier to counsel persons who are mourning before the terminally ill patient dies. Much of the guilt, which often prevents acceptance of death, can be dealt with before death occurs. Survivors who have prepared themselves adequately for the death will usually pass to reestablishment after a relatively brief period of time. If any guilt was left unresolved or unfinished business was not taken care of, however, reaching the stage of reestablishment is more difficult.

One of the ways a mourner may attempt to alleviate this guilt might be through spending large sums of money on the funeral. The expense may make up for unfinished business or the feeling that the bereaved could have prevented the death. David Hendin, a medical and science journalist, in *Death As a Fact of Life* suggests that funerals "serve three major purposes: disposal of the body, aid to the survivors in reorienting themselves after the shock of a loved one's death, and a public acknowledgment of death."[7]

In spite of the adjustment period funerals are supposed to provide, the true adjustment occurs months after the death. It is during this time that the shock and denial begin wearing off and the death becomes more of a reality to the bereaved.

Hendin explains that "when anticipatory grief has occurred, the shock phase of grief is often eliminated because preparations have already been made, sympathies expressed, and grief experienced before death. It is gradually replaced by acceptance of the situation. Although sharp grief was already experienced when the outcome became obvious, an acute stage of grief still comes at the time of death."[8]

Kavanaugh does not deal directly with the grieving of a terminally ill patient, but Kubler-Ross and Hendin do. The various stages in the dying process as described by Kubler-Ross are also part of the grieving process. Kubler-Ross notes, however, that families often block the grieving process of the patient by refusing to accept death. Hendin tells of the case of a terminally ill patient who knows about his impending death, whose wife and daughter refuse to accept the death and expect him to get well. "Mr. P.," he writes, "apparently suffered much more from the feeling that he had disappointed his family than he did from the pain and physical discomfort of his disease. Once his relatives were able to accept the reality of the situation, they stopped trying to urge him back to health and the man was able to die in peace."[9]

Grief after Death

The grief process usually takes a much longer time to work through after a sudden death than after death following a long illness. One woman recently commented that her mother had been ill with cancer for many months. When her mother died, the period it took for her to reestablish herself was quite short. She admitted to being somewhat relieved that the pain was over for her mother. When her father died suddenly of a heart attack, however, it took her three years to accept his death.

The grieving process in an unexpected death usually lasts longer because persons are unprepared for death. The cushion supplied by anticipatory grief has been eliminated. For this reason the shock and denial of death may last longer.

Guilt is a crucial factor in sudden deaths. Persons may inadvertently blame themselves for the death. Survivors of a heart-attack victim may blame themselves for suspecting heart trouble but not consulting a doctor. In accident-related deaths, the survivor may feel guilt in not having found some way of preventing the accident itself. Often children harbor feelings of resentment toward their parents and even secretly wish them "dead." If one of the parents then dies, the child may feel guilt and responsibility.

Guilt resulting from "unfinished business" in living can sometimes be devastating. A couple may have experienced difficulties in their marriage and never resolved these difficulties to their satisfaction. If one dies, the remaining partner may feel hopeless, finding no way to resolve the marital problem with the spouse gone. In a positive relationship, guilt may also be present in the grieving process. Survivors often feel as if they did not "do enough" during the life of a deceased person to show their love and concern.

Death of a Spouse

The grieving process may vary according to family ties and relationships. For the death of a spouse, it is multifaceted. If a younger person loses a spouse, it may take years for the healing process to take place. There may be resentment by the survivor for being left with the responsibilities of family life: raising children, paying bills, maintaining a home. There may also be a sense of unfulfilled promise, commonly heard in the phrase "but we had so much left to do together." For the younger person, however, there is always the possibility of a new beginning with a new spouse.

With older spouses, grieving may take different forms. Although death may be more expected, there is less ability to reestablish new styles of life. Often, older persons in American culture are without other family ties and without means of employment. For this reason, the death of a long relationship may bring on periods of depression, loneliness, and despair.

David Hendin describes what researchers call a "broken heart syndrome" in grieving situations. In studying the deaths of 371 persons, two Welsh researchers found that the death rate among close relatives of the dying person was five percent. Among spouses, those surviving a death showed a twelve-percent death rate themselves in the first year following the death. The researchers discovered that the death rate among widowers was double the death rate among widows. Hendin suggests this may be due to the fact that males are taught to hold in their feelings and cannot grieve as easily as females.

Children and Death

The death of a parent can be a particularly tragic situation for children. Even though children between the ages of three and six often do not perceive death as a finality, they may feel rejected: "He didn't love me; that's why he died." Children below the age of ten often create unreal fantasies regarding the death of a parent.

Typically, relatives are not truthful with the child. Dr. Kubler-Ross says of this approach, "Children are excluded from the planning and sharing of sadness on the pretext that it would be too much for them. But the result is not protection. They are denied a potentially beautiful experience that can unify and strengthen a family." It is healthy for children to remain in the home where a fatality has stricken, according to Kubler-Ross. To be included in the discussion "gives them the feeling that they are not alone in the grief and gives them the comfort of shared responsibility and shared mourning. It prepares them gradually and helps them view death as a part of life, an experience which may help them grow and mature."[10]

Children should be encouraged to express their feelings about a death in the family. A child may also pass through the stages of grief and should be permitted to work through guilt and reestablish ties with life.

The psychiatrist Gregory Rochlin studies a group of children between the ages of three and five by observing their play through a one-way mirror and listening to them through hidden microphones. Death, he concluded, was commonly part of a child's play, entering into games at many levels, but it was never final.[11] Before the age of seven, children are frightened of death, but they are not convinced that it applies to them. After seven, children are capable of perceiving death on a more mature level. It is at this time that parents play an important role in helping children accept death. Earl A. Grollman gives these don'ts for parents:

1. Don't explain death in fairy-tale terms.

2. Don't tell the child what you yourself do not accept.

3. Avoid using symbols that the child cannot understand. A child might be deeply troubled by the statement that "God took Daddy away because He wants the best in Heaven."

4. Don't equate illness with death or equate death with sleep. The child's prayer that includes the well-known lines "If I die before I wake" is both bad psychology and bad theology and could create a pathological fear of bedtime.[12]

Older children come to terms with death in a way that is less painful, and their suffering may not be as acute as that of adults since children have fewer emotional ties and less responsibility.

The death of a child is one of the most difficult to work through. Generally, this death carries with it the greatest amount of anger and resentment. The typical feeling is that life has been wasted and dreams unfulfilled. Very often, parents attempt to keep from a child the knowledge of approaching death. Evidence seems to indicate, however, that children often sense their own impending death but keep this knowledge from their parents in order to protect them. As a result, children may die alone.

Jackson's Grief Triangle

Dr. Edgar Jackson, a Methodist minister who has written extensively on grief therapy, outlines three ways in which mourning can be made more effective or creative. He recommends talking out, feeling out, and acting out one's grief.[13] In the talking-out stage, persons should be encouraged to talk about their grief and express their feelings. Moments of panic, dizziness, and hysteria are some of the symptoms of true grief. When these feelings are ventilated or shared with others, they are less frightening. Despite the belief that the bereaved want to be left alone, they want to talk about their grief with people who care. Feeling out is a cathartic experience for the grieving. This was the function of the ancient Wailing Wall in Jerusalem where people could weep unashamedly and tear their hair. Today society expects those grieving to be stoic and brave; a public display of deep feeling is a source of embarrassment. As a result, feelings are suppressed and lead to depression. Acting out, the third side of Jackson's grief triangle, is a natural extension of feelings. Sheer physical activity gives us some control over our emotions, as is evidenced by the ancient custom of rending one's clothes to express grief.

Describe ways persons can talk out, feel out, and act out feelings of grief.

In John Gunther's book, *Death Be Not Proud*, his wife describes her feelings about the death of their son and shares her grief with parents of living children:

Today, when I see parents impatient or tired or bored with their children, I wish I could say to them, "But they are alive, think of the wonder of that!" They may be a care and a burden, but think, they are alive! You can touch them—what a miracle! You don't have to hold back sudden tears when you see just a headline about the Yale-Harvard game because you know your boy will never see the Yale-Harvard game, never see the house in Paris he was born in, never bring home his girl, and you will not hand down your jewels to his bride and will have no grandchildren to play with and spoil. Your sons and daughters are alive. Think of that—not dead but alive: "Exult and sing."[14]

Throughout life there are many forms of dying—and as many forms of grieving. Each person grieves over the loss of a relationship, outgrowing the dependency on parents, leaving a place considered home. Learning about death also means learning how to grieve creatively, for without the freedom to grieve there can be no newness. Learning to grieve is learning how to reestablish our ties with life, freeing ourselves from the undue mourning of the past into the newness of the moment and the promise of new beginnings.

Exercises

Write the letter of the stage in the grief process beside the statements that best illustrates it.

a. shock
b. disorganization
c. volatile emotions
d. guilt
e. loss and loneliness
f. relief
g. reestablishment

1. A person reacts inappropriately to situations and should postpone important decisions until later.

2. The full impact of the person's death leaves another alienated and isolated.

3. The bereaved experiences the desire to be involved with life again.

4. This stage is closely associated with Kubler-Ross' anger stage.

5. The bereaved experiences a feeling of peace that the departed one is out of pain.

6. The bereaved idealizes the dead person's past and feels responsible for failures.

7. A person blocks the reality of what has been learned about a death.

Write the initials A (anticipatory), G (grief after death), or S (sudden death) to indicate the type of grieving described.

8. Margaret was saddened by the thought that her mother was well into her seventies and only had a few years to live.

9. Mr. Hendrick went into shock when he learned that his wife had died that evening in an automobile accident.

10. The family talked with the doctor for hours after the death of their father.

Circle the letter that best answers the question or completes the statement about grief.

11. According to Hendin, in sudden death
  a. the shock phase of grief is eliminated
  b. the grief process takes a longer time to work through
  c. the cushion supplied by anticipatory grief has been eliminated
  d. b and c

12.   Of the following statements, which best represents a situation where guilt is related to grief?
    a. A heart attack kills a spouse and the partner survives.
    b. Child's parent dies after child wishes he were "dead."
    c. Couple never resolves marital difficulties, and one of them dies.
    d. all of the above

13.   The research of two Welsh psychologists on the deaths of 371 persons showed that
    a. the death rate among close relatives of the dying person was 5 percent
    b. the death rate among widowers was three times as high as among widows
    c. because of conditioning, males cannot grieve as easily as females
    d. none of the above

14.   Research has discovered that in the death of a parent
    a. a child up to the age of ten creates unreal fantasies
    b. children between three and six do not feel rejected
    c. the typical approach of relatives is to be truthful with a child about death
    d. a and b

Turn to the last page of this book to check your answers.

Open-ended Exercises

1.   Group Facilitator: Close your eyes and imagine that you have left this room. Someone stops you, gently takes you aside, and tells you that someone very close to you has died. Who might have died? Think about your reactions and the feelings you might experience during the next twenty-four hours. What would you do?

Members of the group should close their eyes and listen to the group facilitator. After a few minutes' silence, open your eyes and try to express your feelings to the group.

2.   The class should select members to role-play Kavanaugh's stages in the grief process. One student should play a husband who has recently lost his wife. Another student should play a close friend, and a third a minister. The student who is playing the bereaved husband should role-play each of the seven stages in the grief process, with the friend and minister helping him, in a series of seven short vignettes.

3.   Shirley is fifty years old and is married to Bob, a business executive. They have a married daughter, who is twenty-four. Their son, Jim, was recently killed in an accident. Jim had been drinking and arguing about it with Shirley;

then he drove off in anger. A few minutes later Jim had an accident, in which he was instantly killed. Shirley feels guilty because of the circumstances of Jim's death; her anger about his drinking led to the fatal accident.

Since the expression and resolution of grief reasonably soon after the loss is important, what would you do to help Shirley (a) express her grief, and (b) overcome her feelings of guilt?

4. Write your answers to the following questions; then discuss the answers in the group.

a. If you had a terminal illness, would you want to be told? If so, by whom?

b. In what kind of a situation would you feel relief over someone's death?

c. If a child experienced a death in the family, how would you deal with the child's mourning?

d. Why is guilt deepest after a sudden death? How would you deal with this guilt if you were a counselor?

e. How can you determine when an individual has completed the grieving process?

f. What are the advantages and disadvantages of anticipatory grief?

g. What kind of advice would you give to a parent who has lost a young child through death?

h. How do families block the grieving process of terminally ill family members?

i. What are the effects of a death-denying culture on mourners?

j. What events in your life are preparing you to mourn creatively?

Notes

1. Robert E. Kavanaugh, *Facing Death* (Baltimore, Md.: Penguin Books, 1974), p. 107.

2. Ibid., p. 111.

3. Ibid., p. 113.

4. Ibid., p. 119.

5. Ibid., p. 121.

6. G. Gorer, *Death, Grief, and Mourning* (Garden City, N.Y.: Doubleday, 1965).

7. David Hendin, *Death As a Fact of Life* (New York: W. W. Norton, 1973), p. 165.

8. Ibid., p. 176.

9. Ibid., p. 99.

10. Elisabeth Kubler-Ross, *On Death and Dying* (New York: Macmillan, 1974), p. 6.

11. Earl A. Grollman, ed., *Explaining Death to Children* (Boston: Beacon Press, 1967), pp. 51–85.

12. Ibid., pp. 9–12.

13. Edgar Jackson, "On the Wise Management of Grief," paper for a Foundation of Thanatology conference, New York, November 2–3, 1975. See also Edgar Jackson, *You and Your Grief* (New York: Channel, 1961).

14. John Gunther, *Death Be Not Proud* (New York: Harper and Row, 1949), p. 160.

Additional Reading

Anthony, Sylvia. *The Discovery of Death in Childhood and After.* New York: Basic Books, 1972. There is an association between separation and bereavement in childhood and mental illness in later life. Developmental study of how children view death.

Davis, Richard, ed. *Dealing with Death.* Los Angeles: Ethel Percy Andus Gerontology Center, 1972. A practical guide book for coping with death, particularly where older persons are involved.

Eissler, Kurt. *The Psychiatrist and the Dying Patient.* New York: International Universities Press, 1955. Series of interviews and case studies of dying patients.

Evan, Jocelyn. *Living with a Man Who Is Dying.* New York: Taplinger, 1971. Based on personal memories, this study points to the need for honesty in relating to the terminally ill.

Gorer, G. *Death, Grief, and Mourning.* Garden City, N.Y.: Doubleday, 1965. Explains three types of behavior among grieving people: business, mummification, and despair. Excellent study of dynamics of grief.

Grollman, Earl, ed. *Explaining Death to Children.* Boston: Beacon Press, 1967. Volume by outstanding writers from different disciplines who state that it is not the harsh reality of death that undermines the child's stability, but deprivation of the love and understanding of adults.

Jackson, Edgar. *Understanding Grief.* Nashville, Tenn.: Abingdon, 1957. The dynamics of grief are explained, as well as grief and guilt, grief and substitution, and other components of grief.

Kutscher, A. H., and Goldberg, M. *Caring for the Dying Patient and His Family.* H. S. Publishing Corporation, 1973. Excellent study of how to care for a terminally ill patient and his family.

Parkes, Colin Murray. *Bereavement: Studies of Grief in Adult Life.* New York: International Universities Press, 1972. A classic work touching on the grieving process among adults.

Pincus, Lily. *Death and the Family: The Importance of Mourning.* New York: Random House, 1974. The work of a social worker who reflects on her experience reacting to bereavement in families.

Wyschograd, Edith, ed. *The Phenomenon of Death: Faces of Mortality.* New York: Harper and Row, 1973. Observation of those who counseled the dying sheds new light on the psychology of dying patients, allowing people to die in more humane, less isolated manner.

5 The Final Wisdom: Learning from Death

Objectives

1. To explain the similarities and differences between the biological end of life and the existential reality of smaller deaths throughout life

2. To describe the concept of stress and its relationship to death and dying in the views of Hans Selye

3. To discuss Stanley Keleman's distinction between "Little Dying" and "Big Dying" and relate to a group's feelings about small deaths you have experienced

4. To explain why suicide is the most personal form of dying

5. To identify the various meanings that the living can learn from dying and death and relate them to personal experience

6. To record personal meanings gained from the loss of someone close to you and discuss these feelings in a group

Experiencing Death Fully

No poet could write of human mortality and yet capture the everyday realities of life as could William Butler Yeats, of Ireland. A mystic and seeker of spiritual truths, Yeats could still sing of the elements—fire, air, earth, and water—and of the poignancy of death:

> I dreamed that one had died in a strange place
> Near no accustomed hand;
> And they nailed the boards above her face,
> The peasants of the land.[1]

Yeats wrote of the common human themes of life and death, love and hate, man's condition and history; yet he sensed that history was moving toward an end. In his poem "The Second Coming" he wrote:

> The blood-dimmed tide is loosed, and everywhere
> The ceremony of innocence is drowned;
> The best lack all conviction, while the worst
> Are full of passionate intensity.[2]

Yeats' poem entitled "Death" is, perhaps, a key to unlocking how death itself can be the occasion for wisdom, for learning how to live:

> Nor dread nor hope attend
> A dying animal;
> A man awaits his end
> Dreading and hoping all;
> Many times he died,
> Many times he rose again.
> A great man in his pride
> Confronting murderous men
> Casts derision upon
> Supersession of breath;
> He knows death to the bone—
> Man has created death.[3]

We have created death. While this seemingly paradoxical statement at first strikes us as absurd (for, after all, death is an event in which we have no choice), seen in a different light it captures something of the true importance of the dying process. *It is not the experience of death that matters most; it is rather what we do with the experience of death that matters.*

There is no escape from death, although we may believe that in the future our greatest enemy—death—will be eliminated through modern technology. Some may even elect to put their bodies in "deep freeze" to await the day when medical science is prepared to cure their fatal illnesses. The medical profession may forestall death and keep patients in the twilight zone between life and death for months. But, for all the advances, death is still the victor. Death is a biological fact. It cannot be avoided finally, although it can be temporarily detained.

But what is not so certain is how we die. To "die with dignity" may mean that we die as we choose, that our death stands not as a negation of our life but as a final affirmation. The advent of modern technology, which can ease the pain of death, can also add to our slavery by removing our freedom to die as we choose.

Existentially, to die is the final culmination of our living. What we do with the experience of death is, after all, the last frontier of our humanity. In a real sense, each person creates his or her own death. Although technology seeks to remove that level of personal responsibility, death is, as Kubler-Ross notes, the "final stage of growth." And, equally important, we must come to understand that dying is not a reality evident only at the end of life, but present from the beginning of life. There is a story about Plato on his deathbed. Asked by a friend to summarize his great life's work, *The Dialogues*, Plato responded: "Practice dying."

Death, the final separation from our living, follows a long series of smaller deaths. Smaller deaths may, in fact, provide the initial human experiences for our termination. There is wisdom to be gained from consideration of our death, and not merely morbid, hopeless wisdom. In contemplating his own death, the poet Ted Rosenthal learns of life:

> But it turns out that you can live a lifetime in a day; you can live a lifetime in a moment; you can live a lifetime in a year—so that, to the extent they can prolong your life, dying is not a lie. . . . I don't think people are afraid of death. What they are afraid of is the incompleteness of their life.[4]

The Role of Stress

Dr. Hans Selye, a medical researcher and author, offers a unique theory of living that appears to bind together the concepts of death and life. According to Dr. Selye, *stress* is the major cause of the wear and tear of life. The reaction to stress he calls the General Adaptation syndrome. In adapting to any stress situation, there are three phases that the organism undergoes: alarm reaction (initial response), the state of resistance, and the stage of exhaustion. Only the most extreme stress leads to exhaustion, which eventually leads to death.

Normally, one might suppose that over a period of time in the life of any individual the stress of life would provide the occasion for death—the body as a machine would simply run out of the energy necessary to cope with stress. At this point Dr. Selye makes a rather startling discovery:

> Among all my autopsies (and I have performed quite a few), I have never seen a man who died of old age. In fact, I do not think anyone has ever died

of old age yet. . . . We invariably die because one vital part has worn out too early in proportion to the rest of the body. Life, the biologic chain that holds our parts together, is only as strong as its weakest link. When this breaks—no matter which vital link it be—our parts can no longer be held together as a single living being.[5]

In other words, death does not take place at the end of life; it begins with life itself and is a process of disintegration rather than a final dissolution.

From his analysis of stress and life, Dr. Selye derives various philosophical approaches to existence to cope with stress. He agrees with Ernest Becker that egotism is the basic thrust of individual life. In the course of evolution, however, cells found it necessary to cooperate for survival, even at times to sacrifice egotism for the benefit of the whole. In learning to rely more on one another, Dr. Selye believes, we learn better how to cope with stress—and with final exhaustion, or death. He calls this positive human factor *gratitude*.

Gratitude is the awakening in another person of the wish that I should prosper, because of what I have done for him. It is perhaps the most characteristically human way of assuring security (homeostasis). It takes away the motive for a clash between selfish and selfless tendencies because, by inspiring the feeling of gratitude, I have induced another person to share with me my natural wish for my own well-being.[6]

If the narcissistic need for self-perpetuation is the root of our deep terror of death, then gratitude is one way out of the self-induced wasteland.

Little Dying and Big Dying

Stanley Keleman, a therapist, believes that individuals must learn to live by dying "little deaths." Each moment of life that entails a serious and major life change involves dying. "Discovering our dying," he writes, "is a place of transition, a facing of the unknown and the emerging complexity of new ways of being."[7]

Keleman believes that life is a process of journeying through many small deaths, that growth takes place when we accept deaths that are normal to our personal development and permit ourselves the time to grieve—but then move on to the new. He believes that these small deaths are the crucial experiences that prepare us for the "big death." Facing the unknown after separation or loss causes us to become more self-reliant. "These turning points signal that one way of living is over and a new way is emerging; they are rites of passage in the life."[8] These "turning points," like the onset of adolescence, the first job, the move to a new town, the beginning of a new marriage after divorce, are always accompanied by feelings of dying. "Becoming aware of how to handle turning points is experiencing yourself, is discovering how you live with little dying."[9]

Dying is personal. Because death is both a social reality and a deeply personal experience, learning from death requires individual initiative and a respect for the uniqueness of each solitary life. The social aspects of dying are important in teaching us ways in which our culture prepares us for death and acceptable patterns of death. But we do not die in groups; even in mass deaths, our dying is ours alone.

The most intensely personal form of dying is suicide, and it requires special attention. Freud's initial theory of suicide was that it was transposed murder, an act of vengeance turned away from the object back upon the self.

If death is to our age what sex was to the Victorians—an unmentionable factor in human existence—suicide, as a particular self-induced death, is particularly unmentionable, something that happens only to the old, the weak, the insane. It was Plato, however, who pointed out that suicide can be a rational act for those faced with insufferable pain. The Stoics made suicide the most reasonable exodus out of life for the wise man. Death, they felt, was not an evil but was in conformity with nature; when a painful situation is intolerable and hopeless, suicide prevents a person from being enslaved to life. And if one believes that suicide is an act reserved for the mentally or emotionally disturbed, consider those in history who took their own lives. Such philosophers as Socrates, Zeno, Seneca, and Lucretius were among those who chose death over a life they saw as meaningless or dishonorable. And such people of emotional depth and creativity as Van Gogh, Virginia Woolf, Ernest Hemingway, and Jackson Pollock have also taken their own lives.

Sociologist Emile Durkheim's classic study in 1897 explored the social conditions that engendered suicidal acts. Since that time, social scientists have continued research in the field. Alvarez, in his moving treatise on suicide, concludes: "The psychoanalytic theories of suicide prove, perhaps, only what was already obvious: that the processes which lead a man to take his own life are at least as complex and difficult as those by which he continues to live."[10]

Learning from death entails learning from those who decided to choose the moment and means of their own dying, learning something of the inner logic of suicide. In an age in which our choice of death is each year moved further from our own volition, in which dying becomes a program prescribed by medical technologists, there is something to be learned from those who decisively elect self-destruction.

One might paraphrase the Protestant reformer Martin Luther and say that each person must do his or her own dying, just as each person must do his or her own believing. In a very real and personal sense, dying is individual and solitary. You may be surrounded by friends and you may believe your death is following a universal pattern, but it will be your unique "I" that transpires. Although others may provide support to you, it is only you who can die. Yet lessons learned from others who have died can give meaning to the dying process.

Lessons from Death

Following are ten rather tentative meanings or "lessons" that death and dying impart. The list suggests that rather than denying death, we ought to learn its meaning for our lives. It is somewhat ironic that in our desire to deny death, we deny ourselves the possibilities of humanity and of learning from the most universal and important life experience. To approach death not as the enemy but as the teacher, to understand that knowledge of death has something to say to us now of living, is perhaps the wisdom needed to live. One always hears stories of persons on their deathbeds turning to friends or relatives and remarking: "Oh, I wish I had done it differently; I wish I had known then what I know now." Learning from death while we are yet living provides this opportunity.

1. *Our knowledge of death can impart to us the value of life.* There are those who consider thoughts of death morbid, a sign of mental illness, or unhealthy, and it must be noted that obsessive thoughts of dying can be a sign of other emotional problems. However, a knowledge that life is not forever, that it has limits, can teach us to use our brief portions of time wisely and with love. Kubler-Ross points out that in her work among terminally ill patients, many have "unfinished business" they wish to fulfill before their deaths. The unfinished business may be resolving an old argument with a relative or simply making that trip to Europe, postponed for years. No matter what the business is, death becomes easier when it has been fulfilled.

From the dying it might be learned that our "unfinished business" need not wait until we have only a few months to live. We can learn in the here and now to seek our fulfillment, to live in the richness of the moment. If we knew, as a terminally ill patient knows, that life is measured in months, how might we change what we now are or do things differently?

Because we cannot envision our own death, we tend to think of ourselves as limitless. For this reason, we tend to think of our existence as being open-ended; we think we have forever to complete our work, our dreams, our hopes. But those who face death know that life is limited and that each moment must be counted as a gift.

In summing up her personal views of death, Dr. Kubler-Ross describes how from death we can learn of life:

> I am convinced that these experiences with the reality of death have enriched my life more than any other experiences I have had. Facing death means facing the ultimate question of the meaning of life. If we really want to live, we must have the courage to recognize that life is ultimately very short and that everything we do counts. When it is the evening of our life, we will hopefully have a chance to look back and say: "It was worthwhile because I have really lived."[11]

2. *Understanding death can teach us to respect our human limitations.* The terror of death—and our problems in everyday life—may stem from the fact

that we think too highly of ourselves. In Ernest Becker's view, we are human animals who are hopelessly involved with ourselves; and in this self-concern, the threat of nonbeing, of death, brings on a denial of death itself. The Judeo-Christian heritage attempts to overcome this undue concern for self with a form of self-giving love (*agapé*), which transcends total involvement with the self. Eastern philosophies tend to ascribe to the view that since there is no stable, unified self, the wise man should not fear death.

Understanding death means understanding that there are realities outside our control, over which even our tendencies to hold life and manipulate it have no bearing. To understand that there is an end of our individual existence and that all our attempts to seize life and accumulate possessions come to naught is to be open to humility, accepting the fact that we are finite creatures and not gods. In a sense, then, we live in a state of grace (in theological terms), aware of our limitations and cognizant that in the face of death we must learn to accept.

The myth of contemporary man is that he is finally in control, that through technology nature itself can be tamed and made the servant of humanity. Death confronts this myth and teaches that the universe is more vast than our need to control it and more mysterious than our desire to explain it.

3.   *To understand death, one must finally learn the difference between chronological and qualitative time.* In contemporary culture, we measure history by chronological time; we are creatures of the clock. Time is a sequence measured by hours and dates and events in proper order. So, too, we measure our lives by the clock; we think of our lives as progressing through time from birth to death. But in understanding the dying process, one becomes aware of a different measure—the quality of life. Terminally ill patients are particularly aware that it is not the length of life but what has been done with time that matters most. You can live a lifetime in a moment or a day. Though the scriptures tell of a life of threescore years and ten, it is interesting to note that the New Testament word for life, *zoe*, does not refer to chronological time but to the quality of life.

To know one is going to die is first to be made aware of the brevity of life itself. To know that life is short may require a personal restructuring of values to compress as much living as possible into a shortened time. Ted Rosenthal remarked that after learning he had only a short time to live, he suddenly knew that what he feared was not death but having lived an unfulfilled life. Those who deal with dying patients know situations in which people take on projects during their remaining months they had put off before. A frustrated writer may finally try to write that book he or she has been thinking about for thirty years; an amateur painter may start painting.

To know that we are going to die means that life suddenly can take on a new meaning, measured not by the clock but by the quality of our existence.

4.   *Learning from death means that we must learn to let go of what we consider important, even ourselves.* Buddhism teaches that the root of suffering is our "craving to exist," to accumulate possessions. Individuals tend to have great difficulty in "letting go" of relationships, values, and ideas. In a marriage partners may hang onto the relationship only for fear of what others think and of the insecurity involved in separation. A devoutly religious person may ascribe to old values as a security precaution, fearful of the implications of the new.

The act of dying implies letting go of everything. When you die, all the world dies with you. From those who are dying we learn that finally we must let go, that we can no longer hang onto our values, not to mention our very existences. Death is the final letting go of our craving to exist. Learning from death means that in living we learn to let go of those unimportant values and beliefs that only hinder growth.

Religious philosopher Alan Watts claimed that the certainty of death is an extremely liberating experience. Hanging on to one's ego is self-strangulation, and death is "the greatest opportunity you'll ever have to experience what it's like to let go of yourself."[12] Accepting the reality of death also helps the person to realize how good *now* is and eliminates morbid preoccupation with an uncertain future.

5.   *From the dying, we learn something of the meaning of intimacy.* In working with dying patients, even when they are silent, those in the helping professions have noticed the development of the truly personal life; in facing death, persons tend to seek a degree of intimacy, particularly those who have reached a level of acceptance. For some, this intimacy comes with words; for others, intimacy involves a touch of a hand or simply crying together. In intimacy, defenses are down and we appear to each other as we are, not as we hope others will think we are.

6.   *In death we learn the ultimate significance of silence.* In contemporary times we seem to suffer from noise pollution. Our talk goes on forever. Kubler-Ross talks of a "silence which goes beyond words" in dealing with patients near death. "There is a time in the patient's life," she writes, "when the pain ceases to be, when the mind slips off into a dreamless state, when the need for food becomes minimal and the awareness of the environment all but disappears into darkness."[13]

At this particular moment in the dying process, she says, those in the helping professions must have the strength and love to sit quietly and not talk. "Watching a peaceful death of a human being reminds us of a falling star; one of the million lights in a vast sky that flares up for a brief moment only to disappear into the endless night forever."[14]

In learning from death, we learn there is a language beyond words, in which communication still takes place in all its magnificent mystery.

7.   *The mystery of being is revealed in death because it is beyond our range of normal experience.* In contemporary life, human beings appear to be reduced to their functions and routinized. For this reason, existence seems more of a problem than a process, a question to be solved rather than a mystery to be explored. Death opens us to what the existentialist philosopher Gabriel Marcel calls "ontological mystery." It is that point in human experience at which we bump into ultimate reality. Of course it is impossible to define what Marcel means by mystery, for one cannot use reason to reach mystery; rather, one must participate in the mystery. Death reveals to us dimensions beyond our range of everyday experience; it opens our imaginations to the meaning of life and what possibly might happen after death. We cannot reason our way into death or into what is beyond death. In death's presence we remain in awe of the unknown.

8.   *The final dying process can teach us how to deal with smaller deaths during our lifetime.* Each of us may think of death as the biological end of life, without considering that in another sense death is what we do when living. Our biological death is, in one sense, a final letting go of our physical bodies. But all along life's path we experience smaller deaths, smaller letting-go experiences. For some, this may mean letting go of a significant person or changing jobs; children may experience smaller deaths in moving from a familiar community to another city. In a divorce, one may go through denial, bargaining, anger, depression, and acceptance. These smaller deaths may be preparatory for our final death and serve as learning experiences for that end. To permit ourselves to mourn may provide us a means of grieving when someone we love dies. In this way, learning about death and dying can prepare us for living. And, if possible, from death and dying we may learn that without death there is no new beginning.

9.   *In understanding how a dying person finally reaches acceptance, we may be given a clue as to how we can learn to accept ourselves in the here-and-now.* If patients in pain and suffering can move through denial and depression to some measure of acceptance, then there is hope that those who are living free of pain can move into an acceptance of themselves in the present. If in "letting go" of ourselves now, letting go of our small pains, we can be brought in touch with ourselves and with those we love, our small deaths will not be wasted. Kubler-Ross says that when a patient has accepted death, there is a beauty and peace beyond understanding. That knowledge alone provides hope, for it says that in acceptance—even of small deaths—there is a serenity.

10.   *From death, we may learn that we are individuals, apart from any social roles we have played in life.* In the moment of death we are brought face-to-face with our selves, not the self that has functioned as a lawyer, a housewife, a factory worker, but the self that theologians tell us is revealed only in God's presence. In a nonreligious sense, death strips away the roles we have played thoughout life, leaving only the "I." It may be possible that at the moment of death the unique "I" transcends itself and is gathered up into the source of all being.

These, then, are ten simplified "lessons" to be learned from death and dying. Each person will be able to supply other insights based on individual experiences. But, as Kubler-Ross notes in her workshops, we have much to learn from the dying, if only we will listen.

One could well remark of death with Cesare Pavese: "One learns that the only way to escape from the abyss is to look at it, measure it, sound its depths and go down into it."[15] And, paradoxically enough, in learning of death and dying we may also learn something of life.

Exercises

Write T (true) or F (false) beside each statement about Selye's theory of stress.

1. Stress is a major cause of the wear and tear of life.

2. It is during the alarm reaction stage of the General Adaptation syndrome that death usually occurs.

3. Death does not take place at the end of life but begins with life.

4. One human factor that acts as a resistor to stress is gratitude.

Circle the letter of the phrase that best completes each statement.

5. Plato believed that suicide
   a. is retroflexed anger
   b. is a rational act for those who suffered intolerable pain
   c. prevents a person from being enslaved to life
   d. both b and c

6. The deaths of Van Gogh, Zeno, Seneca, and Socrates show that suicide
   a. is an act reserved for emotionally disturbed persons
   b. can be a heroic act of the will
   c. is a matter for scientific research
   d. all of the above

7. According to Kubler-Ross, the unfinished business of a dying patient refers to
   a. unfinished work
   b. unresolved guilt feelings
   c. unexpressed feelings for loved ones
   d. all of the above

8. The reality of time that terminally ill patients have learned is that
   a. living a long life is important
   b. the quality of life matters most
   c. life is measured by its donation, not duration
   d. both b and c

9. Watts believed that death is a liberating experience because
   a. death frees a person from self-strangulation of the ego
   b. persons are delivered from suffering
   c. death frees persons from enslavement to other persons
   d. both a and c

10. One of the insights we learn from the dying person is
    a. the meaning of intimacy
    b. an understanding of life's priorities
    c. the significance of silence
    d. the importance of individuality

Turn to the last page of this book to check your answers.

Open-ended Exercises

1. Although you may never have had a "near death" experience, everyone has experienced some "small death." Choose any of these situations of "small deaths" and role-play them.

a. A twelve-year-old son experiences the loss of his father, who has just separated from his mother.

b. A girl, age twenty, finds her engagement is suddenly over because of her fiancé's involvement with another girl.

c. A teacher, after twenty years of service to an elementary school, is forced to retire.

d. A wife confronts the reality of a divorce after twenty-five years of marriage.

e. A sixteen-year-old boy finds that his father has been transferred to another state, and he must leave all of his lifelong friends.

2. What personal meanings do you feel can be gained from exploring death and dying? If you have experienced the loss of someone close to you, what have you learned from that loss? Discuss these feelings with a group.

Notes

1. M. L. Rosenthal, ed., *Selected Poems and Two Plays of William Butler Yeats* (New York: Macmillan, 1962), pp. 14–15

2. Ibid., p. 91.

3. Ibid., p. 123.

4. Ted Rosenthal, *How Could I Not Be Among You?* (New York: Avon, 1975), p.53.

5. Hans Selye, *The Stress of Life* (New York: McGraw Hill, 1956), p. 276.

6. Ibid., p. 285.

7. Stanley Keleman, *Living Your Dying* (New York: Random House, 1974), p. 23.

8. Ibid., p. 21.

9. Ibid., p. 25.

10. A. Alvarez, *The Savage God* (New York: Bantam Books, 1973), p. 23.

11. Elisabeth Kubler-Ross, *Death: The Final Stage of Growth* (Englewood Cliffs, N.J.: Prentice-Hall, 1975), pp. 125–126.

12. Alan Watts, "Psychotherapy and Eastern Religion," *Journal of Transpersonal Psychology* 6 (1974), p. 25.

13. Elisabeth Kubler-Ross, *On Death and Dying* (New York: Macmillan, 1970), p. 276.

14. Ibid., p. 276.

15. Alvarez, *Savage God*, p. 136.

Additional Reading

Alvarez, A. *The Savage God.* New York: Bantam Books, 1973. Meaningful insight into suicide from a personal, existential point of view. Suicide is seen as the end of a long experience, an emptiness so isolated and violent that it surrenders.

Beauvoir, Simon de. *A Very Easy Death.* New York: G.P. Putman's Sons, 1966. Description of how the death of a loved one is hard to accept, since one has no other point of reference.

Hinton, J. M. *Dying.* Baltimore, Md.: Penguin Press, 1967. Rational and irrational emotions associated with death are described by a psychiatrist involved with patients suffering from incurable diseases. Author tries to take away the "frightening magnetism" of contemplating death and explains how death teaches us about life.

Keleman, Stanley, *Living Your Dying.* New York: Random House, 1974. Explored from the stance of transpersonal psychology, death is a necessary part of experiencing meaning in life.

Neale, Robert E. *The Art of Dying.* New York: Harper and Row, 1973. Facilitates movement from death to life, as awareness of death leads to greater awareness of life.

Reimer, Jack. *Jewish Reflections on Death.* New York: Schocken, 1974. With a foreword by Kubler-Ross, this anthology on readings from Jewish writers explains death as seen by a people who have faced annihilation. Authors argue that Judaism offers a realistic view of death and concern for ethical decisions in this life.

Ruitenbeek, Hendrik. *The Interpretation of Death.* New York: Jason Aronson, 1973. Series of articles on death and mourning stressing that death makes persons confront the realities of life.

6 Beyond Death

Objectives

1. To explain how the idea of immortality arose in human culture

2. To define and describe Lifton and Olson's five modes or categories of immortality

3. To describe the Christian doctrine of life after death as survival of the person

4. To suggest arguments for and against the concept of immortality

5. To explain the implications of the work of Kubler-Ross, Noyes, and Moody to the concept of immortality

6. To explore the positive and negative implications of theories of immortality to life in the here-and-now

7. To describe your personal feelings about immortality on a questionnaire and participate in a group experience in which these feelings are discussed

The Concept of Immortality

Some writers in the field of the history of religion claim that the yearning for immortality is so prevalent among world religions that it is almost universal. But the scientific bias of the age looks askance at the concept of immortality, essentially because it does not appear to be a subject open to scientific proof.

In their book on death, Robert Lifton and Eric Olson conclude that "it is possible to look at all human history as a record of man's diverse answers to these questions of immortality."[1] Dostoevsky, the Russian writer and philosopher, concluded that there were only three great ideas in Western culture: God, freedom, and immortality. He wrote, "The idea of immortality is life itself, the definitive formulation and the first source of the truth and integrity of conscience."[2] Dostoevsky saw in immortality a reason for believing in the absolute value of human life; either man is an immortal spirit with a destiny beyond this life, or he is an empirical object with no lasting value beyond the material world.

The post-Freudian thinker Ernest Becker calls immortality a universal passion. "The urge to immortality," he writes, "is not a simple reflex of the death-anxiety but a reaching out by one's whole being toward life."[3] What psychoanalysts call identification, he feels, is nothing more than the natural urge to join in the overwhelming powers that transcend us, to move beyond the limitations of the dying animal and our bodies. The life force, Becker feels, seeks to expand beyond the limitations of the here-and-now, to move into those dimensions that fill the pages of mystical literature.

William Wordsworth, the English poet, saw a continuation of life beyond death—and even life before birth. In his poem "Intimations of Immortality" he writes:

> Our birth is but a sleep and a forgetting;
> The Soul that rises with us, our life's star,
> Hath had elsewhere its setting,
> And cometh from afar. . . . [4]

Categories of Immortality

Lifton and Olson describe five modes or categories of immortality: biological, creative, theological, natural, and experiential.

Biological immortality is the most easily expressed. It implies simply that we survive through our children and their children, throughout generations. This category of immortality is symbolized by the reproductive cells that are passed along from parent to child.

The *creative model of immortality* implies the notion that a person "lives on" through his or her contributions. Traditionally, this concept has been associated with the artist, who hopes to live on through music or art. Becker calls this the enlightenment view of immortality. Some theorists say it was this form of immortality that most concerned Freud, who aspired to creating his own immortality through his contributions to Western thought.

Theological immortality is described in the history of religions, which shows how various world religions have prescribed paths of life to conquer death and reflects their views of the afterlife.

Natural immortality suggests that persons are interconnected with nature and that nature itself will never die.

Experiential immortality depends solely on a psychological state. Experiences of going beyond life in the here-and-now are reported by those who use drugs or practice various semi-Eastern meditative philosophies. Persons using other approaches, such as astral projection, also report such out-of-body experiences.

Doctrines of Life after Death

Immortality may also be described in terms of two broad doctrines of survival after death prevalent in world religions and philosophies. One such doctrine, which might be called *soul body theory* of immortality, originated in the East and passed into Western culture through Plato. In this theory the soul is thought to be eternal, while the body is substance of a lesser nature. The soul dwells in the body only as a temporary resting place. According to one Eastern religion, the soul goes through an endless series of rebirths (*samsara*); in other religions, the soul's rebirths are governed by *karma* so that actions on the material plane govern rebirth into the new plane. Plato believed in an ever-changing world of matter and a more permanent spiritual world. In the soul-body theory of immortality, living beyond death is not an issue; what is important is that the wise person orders life in this world knowing that the soul will continue into eternity or return again to earth.

A second doctrine of immortality might be called *personal survival*. In this view, the departed soul exists as a more or less pale copy or ghost of the living person. Some individuals who claim to be in tune with the departed hold seances to communicate with the dead. Many of the best-sellers on immortality seem to take this approach, and some authors provide "records" of conversations with the dead. One American medium, Arthur Ford, conducted numerous seances with seemingly remarkable results. His most famous case was a televised session in which Ford communicated personal information between Bishop James Pike of the Episcopal Church and the bishop's deceased son.

The Judeo-Christian heritage seems somewhat mixed on the question of immortality. In some cases, the Hebrews inherited the view that the soul did not cease to exist but either departed to the shadowy world of Sheol or else returned to God. Christian theologians often seem divided between this concept of the immortality of the soul and the concept of the resurrection of the body.

For some Christian thinkers, the view that the total person is resurrected removes the unnecessary dualism between the belief that the soul is immortal and the belief that the body is resurrected. This comprehensive view denies (a) a literal resuscitation of the present body, that is, an actual resurrection of the particles of matter that form our present bodies, and (b) that life after death is limited to an immortality of the "mind." The life beyond must involve the whole person so that our total experiences now in the body are thereby preserved.

One of the strongest proponents of the concept of immortality was the Spanish philosopher and author Miguel de Unamuno. For Unamuno, immortality was not an abstract topic, but the very essence of what life is about. And it is not the immortality of the soul of which he speaks, but the continuation of the total personality, the "man of flesh and bone." To the question "What is Man?" Unamuno would answer, "the hunger of immortality."

Unamuno believed that Christian thinkers had limited the idea of immortality by a narrow conception of "soul." For Unamuno, the soul was equated with the total person, that is, man's being.

> The Hellenic idea of immortality was a caricature of the true immortality. . . . Instead of detaching itself from the body, freeing itself in a Platonic manner, . . . or living in the body as if it were outside it, this soul dragged the body after it toward eternal life, making the body a "spiritual" reality.[4]

New Testament writers used the ambiguous term *spirit-body* to describe this phenomenon. Thus, the Christian doctrine of life after death actually means that the *person* survives: there is fullness of personal existence in life after death. Rather than providing any specific kind of life after death, the Christian seems to arrive at a conclusion of faith in that the ultimate reality (God) gathers unto himself all.

Arguments against the entire concept of immortality are innumerable. George Bernard Shaw once wrote, "What man is capable of the insane self-conceit of believing that an eternity of himself would be tolerable even to himself?"[6]

Freud was particularly harsh on the theory of immortality. In his book *Future of an Illusion,* he attacked the notion of immortality as an illusion that takes human beings away from the business of living. Becker suggests, however, that Freud launched this attack with his fingers crossed under his desk. "As you fear that life in this dimension may not count, may not have any real meaning, you relieve your anxiety by being especially scornful of the very thing that you wish for most," he writes of Freud.[7] Karl Marx also viewed the whole religious notion of immortality as a diversion to take men's minds off the problems of this world.

Near-Death Experiences

Of tremendous importance is the research of physicians and psychiatrists who work among dying patients. What can be learned from these persons concerning life after death?

In her workshops on death and dying, Dr. Kubler-Ross flatly says "There is no death"—a strange statement for a scientist, an individual who claims not to ascribe to any particular theological stance. For a number of years she has been interviewing individuals who were declared legally "dead" and then restored to life. Each of the individuals was interviewed separately and without knowledge of what the others had said. Although the results are as yet unpublished in book form by Kubler-Ross, these are some of her findings as she notes them in her workshops:

1.   Persons, while they were "dead," felt a sense of wholeness, of peace, of tranquility, of being "at home."

2.   Most remembered observing their bodies after death. For example, some recalled watching doctors attempt to restore their lives.

3.   Immediately after their deaths, many of those who had "died" were greeted by a loved one "on the other side" or, if they were religious, by a historical religious figure.

4.   All of those interviewed felt anger when they were brought back to life and restored.

The work of Noyes (University of Iowa College of Medicine) on near-death experiences also provides some innovative approaches to the issue of immortality. In studying individual recollections of near-death experiences, Noyes found that the psychological patterns of the person could be broken down into three chronological divisions: resistance, review, and transcendence. The individual first violently resists and struggles against what is happening. If the threat of death is not removed, the individual may surrender to a feeling of passive resignation; in this state the person goes through a "life review" stage and watches his life ebb and flow. The common perception is of life flowing by, of watching a rapidly moving filmstrip in which images of the past flash before the person's mind. Noyes says about thirty-three percent of those interviewed passed through this life-review stage.

About twenty-five percent of the persons interviewed entered the third stage, transcendence. Here the individuals feel as if they have passed beyond the boundaries of the self. The comments of a Swiss geology professor, Albert von St. Gallen-Heim, who had nearly been killed in a 66–foot fall from a mountain peak, illustrate the feelings attached to transcendence: "Everything was transfigured, as though by a heavenly light, and everything was beautiful without grief, without anxiety, and without pain. I became ever more surrounded by a splendid blue heaven with delicate roselike and violet cloudlets."[8]

Was this experience typical? Noyes interviewed, over the next twenty-five years, many other survivors of Alpine falls, asking them all the same question: "What was your experience in the 'last' seconds of life?" Later included were victims of railroad disasters, rescued victims of drowning, and others who had felt they were facing death. The findings confirmed Noyes' previous observation: The moment of death is not to be feared, but embraced. The image of light and beauty and the feeling of tremendous peace were reported also to Kubler-Ross by the individuals interviewed.

The physician Raymond A. Moody, Jr., in reviewing 150 near-death experiences, reports findings similiar to those of Kubler-Ross and Noyes. On the basis of interviews with these persons, Moody constructed a brief, theoretical model of the type of experiences reported:

> A man is dying and, as he reaches the point of greatest physical distress, he hears himself pronounced dead by his doctor. He begins to hear an uncomfortable noise, a loud ringing or buzzing, and at the same time feels himself moving very rapidly through a long dark tunnel. After this, he suddenly finds himself outside of his own physical body, but still in the immediate physical environment, and he sees his own body from a distance, as though he is a spectator. He watches the resuscitation attempt from this unusual vantage point and is in a state of emotional upheaval.
>
> After a while, he collects himself and becomes more accustomed to his odd condition. He notices that he still has a "body," but one of a very different nature and with very different powers from the physical body he has left behind. Soon other things begin to happen. Others come to meet and to help him. He glimpses the spirits of relatives and friends who have already died, and a loving, warm spirit of a kind he has never encountered before—a being of light—appears before him. This being asks him a question, nonverbally, to make him evaluate his life and helps him along by showing him a panoramic, instantaneous playback of the major events of his life. At some point he finds himself approaching some sort of barrier or border, apparently representing the limit between earthly life and the next life. Yet, he finds that he must go back to the earth, that the time for his death has not yet come. At this point he resists, for by now he is taken up with his experiences in the afterlife and does not want to return. He is overwhelmed by intense feelings of joy, love, and peace. Despite his attitude, though, he somehow reunites with his physical body and lives.[9]

Based on his interviews, Moody is convinced that his findings have great implications for how persons should live their lives in the here-and-now, but he attempts to view his findings cautiously. He suggests that there may be three general "explanations" for the experiences uncovered in near-death situations: supernatural, natural, and psychological. The supernatural explanation assumes that there is an afterlife, which is somehow part of the divine nature of the universe. The natural explanation supposes that near-death experiences can be explained either in terms of the expanding nature of the mind itself or of various biochemical reactions of the body. The psychological explanation would propose that either conscious lying or unconscious embellishment might have taken place.

Moody seems to end with as many questions as answers.

> Enlightenment on this subject is needed by members of many professions and academic fields. It is needed by the physician who has to deal with the fears and hopes of the dying patient and by the minister helping others to face death. It is needed also by psychologists and psychiatrists, because in order to devise a workable and reliable method for the therapy of emotional disturbances they need to know what the mind is and whether it can exist apart from the body.[10]

Implications of Immortality

Arthur Ford, who was a Christian minister as well as a prominent medium, comments categorically:

> A general emancipation from the searing grip of this most fearsome of all dreads would free tremendous human energies for all the creative tasks of life. And there is no rational reason for delaying any longer a general enjoyment of this immeasurable benefit. A hundred years of careful research has established the essential fact of survival to the satisfaction of all who approach the evidence with a free mind.[11]

The American psychologist William James was a pioneer in psychical research and concerned himself critically with the pragmatic implications of human immortality. In his book *Varieties of Religious Experience*, he encouraged an understanding of religious realities as "windows" into an unseen world. While James never reached a firm conviction on the question of immortality, he consistently argued for the vital importance of the inquiry into life beyond death. In his *Human Immortality*, a small book based on a 1898 lecture at Harvard University, James suggested that perhaps the brain acts as a transmitter rather than an originator of mental processes, so that the deceased might possibly be able to carry on a transphysical existence. In this book James writes: "I wish to go on record for . . . the presence, in the midst of all the humbug, of really supernormal knowledge."[12] By this James was saying that there are forms of knowing outside the scientific method of inquiry, and that the exploration into "supernormal knowledge" ought to be thoroughly investigated.

Somewhere between those who seem to speak daily with the dead—and refuse to consider that their excursions into psychic phenomena may be nothing more than travels into unexplored regions of the human psyche—and those who, in the name of reason, refuse to consider the possibility of life after death, there lies a middle ground. This middle ground may be as uncomfortable to the traditional religious person as it is to the skeptical scientist. *For the middle position implies that we do not yet know enough about the subject of immortality to provide any final solution to the question of life after death, but that the question itself is of ultimate and far-reaching significance, resting at the very heart of the meaning of life and human destiny.*

For the religiously dogmatic individual who believes there are already "highway maps to the afterlife," the admission of the need for further exploration will open up new methods of inquiry—which may contradict established teachings. But in the history of world religions, every new idea and belief is revolutionary and comes with a strikingly novel power. For the trained rationalist, the whole question of immortality suggests a return to the days of the Inquisition. But the revolutionary truths of today are the established truths of tomorrow; and how is it possible to know any truth without first being open to the possibility of its existence?

The inquiry may, of course, fail to document or deny the reality of immortality. The real question concerning immortality, however, is one that might be asked by the existentialist: what would the existence of immortality mean for life now? How would we order our lives, for example, if we knew that our existence did not end with death? Be assured that there are no easy answers to these questions.

Some philosophers would argue that without immortality, without any continuation of life, existence becomes absurd—and we are reduced to finite creatures struggling pathetically and without meaning in an insane world. Dostoevsky, for example, would argue that without immortality, we are reduced to materialistic machines without final accountability for our actions. Immanuel Kant, one of the greatest of all philosophers, argued that immortality was necessary because justice was never completed in this life.

Other thinkers would counter that immortality provides us with another illusion, that it robs life in the here-and-now of its meaning—and opens human beings to manipulation by institutions that use the threat of hell as a whip to force individuals into acceptable thought and behavior patterns. Would we live richer and fuller lives, knowing that death is not the end? Or would we manipulate each other or ignore the suffering of the present life while concentrating on the benefits of the next?

Noyes suggests that the concept of self-transcendence is extremely valuable in working through life problems. The suggestion is made that perhaps some individuals can be guided through the sequence of ego-death and rebirth. Keleman believes individuals need to work through ambivalent feelings in every "little dying" encountered in life. He further suggests that the human being has a built-in genetic program for dying that is a part of the total development of the personality. What is at stake is nothing less than the transformation of human personality from stages of fear and denial to stages of acceptance and fulfillment.

One need not ascribe to any particular concept of immortality, but the realization that life may not end with death can have a revolutionary impact on the way in which we order our lives. Moody concludes that if there is any truth in the experiences of those who have undergone near-death situations, "then it would be true that we cannot fully understand this life until we catch a glimpse of what lies beyond it."[13]

Exercises

Beside each statement write the letter that identifies the type of immortality described: B (biological), C (creative), T (theological), N (natural), or E (experiential).

1. He completed his last book of poetry as a testament to life for future generations.

2. The oceans and the mountains live on forever.

3. Listening to Bach, she was aware that suddenly she was beyond time and herself.

4. "The kingdom of heaven is coming soon," said the prophet.

5. He thought about his grandparents and their grandparents and the many generations of his ancestors.

Write T (true) or F (false) beside each statement about life after death.

6. Hebrews believe that the soul departs to the shadowy world of Sheol or returns to God.

7. The Greek concept of immortality includes a survival of the total person after death.

8. Unamuno felt that the Christian writers had limited immortality to a narrow conception of the soul.

9. The proper view of immortality, according to Unamuno, is that only the spiritual aspect of man lives forever.

10. The Christian doctrine of life after death states that the total person survives.

11. Freud thought the idea of immortality was an illusion.

12. Unamuno believed that only the soul survived death.

Circle the letter of the phrase that completes each statement.

13. According to Kubler-Ross, patients who were declared legally "dead" and then restored to life
    a. felt a sense of wholeness and peace
    b. were greeted by loved ones on the other side
    c. felt anger when restored to life
    d. all of the above

14. On the basis of her experience and research, Kubler-Ross believes that
    a. life after death remains an unknown quantity
    b. there is no death
    c. the soul is reincarnated in another form
    d. there is no afterlife

15. In studying recollections of near-death experiences, Noyes found
    a. over 80 percent of individuals transcended death
    b. no common experiences
    c. some persons passed through a life-review process
    d. most persons felt fear and frustration

16. Moody's model of the near-death experience includes
    a. terrible, prolonged isolation
    b. encounter with a "being of light"
    c. fear of the unknown
    d. lack of contact on the other side

Turn to the last page of this book to check your answers.

Open-ended Exercises

1. Each member of the group should write an original poem or essay expressing feelings about or experiences with death. Students who prefer to work with visual materials rather than words may choose to make paintings or collages. The poems, essays, or paintings should be submitted anonymously, and each member of the group should read or present one selection of the material to the group. The group will then try to decide which of its members wrote the poem or essay or did the painting.

2. The question "Is there an afterlife?" should be asked, and each member of the group should respond by saying "Yes, because_____." or "No, because_____." or "I don't know because_____."

3. Members of the group should write short answers to these questions.

a. Would you want to live forever?

b. Do you feel there is a part of you that will not die? In what part of your body is your unique "I" located?

c. What kind of evidence would you accept as proof that there is a life after death? How would you go about collecting such evidence?

d. Have you ever had a near-death experience? What was it like?

e. If there is personal immortality, do you think persons will be more, or less, concerned about life in the here-and-now? Why?

Notes

1. Robert J. Lifton and Eric Olson, *Living and Dying* (New York: Bantam Books, 1975), p. 53.

2. Nicolas Berdyaev, *Dostoevsky* (New York: Living Age Books, 1960), p. 105.

3. Ernest Becker, *The Denial of Death* (New York: The Free Press, 1973), p. 152.

4. Mark Van Doren, ed., *William Wordsworth* (New York: The Modern Library, 1950), p. 543.

5. Jose Mora, *Unamuno: A Philosophy of Tragedy* (Berkeley: University of California Press, 1962), p. 53.

6. Geddes MacGregor, *Introduction to the Philosophy of Religion* (Boston: Houghton Mifflin, 1959), p. 198.

7. Ernest Becker, *The Denial of Death* (New York: The Free Press, 1973), p. 121.

8. Charles A. Garfield, "Consciousness Alternation and Fear of Death," *Journal of Transpersonal Psychology*, vol. 7, no. 2 (1975), p. 171.

9. Raymond A. Moody, Jr., *Life after Life* (Covington, Ga.: Mockingbird Books, 1976), pp. 23–24.

10. Ibid., p. 124.

11 Arthur Ford, *Unknown but Known* (New York: The New American Library, 1968), p. 70.

12. Gardner Murphy and Robert O. Ballau, *William James on Psychical Research* (New York: The Viking Press, 1960), p. 322

13. Moody, *Life after Life*, p. 125.

Additional Reading

Aldwinckle, Russell. *Death in the Secular City*. London: George Allan and Unwin, Ltd., 1972. Theological discussion of life after death, including views of Jesus and the doctrines of immortality and resurrection.

Cullman, Oscar. *Immortality of the Soul or Resurrection of the Body*. New York: Macmillan, 1974. Author distinguishes between the Greek view of life after death as liberation from the prison of the body, and the Judeo-Christian view of resurrection of the total person.

Cousins, Ewert H., ed. *Hope and the Future of Man*. Philadelphia: Fortress Press, 1972. Report of a conference involving well-known theologians, including John Cobb, Jurgen Moltmann, Wolfhart Pannenberg, in which several views are presented.

Cousins, Norman. *The Celebration of Life*. New York: Harper and Row, 1974. Engaging Socratic dialogue that builds a philosophy of optimism; immortality based on the "brotherhood of man."

Dempsey, David. *The Way We Die: An Investigation of Death and Dying in America Today*. New York: Macmillan, 1975. Evidence for survival after death is presented from the work of William James and William McDougall in psychic research.

Ford, Arthur. *The Life Beyond Death*. New York: G.P. Putnam's Sons, 1971. Last written words of Ford, the trance medium, including belief that biological death is not final, but survival after death releases energies for creative tasks of life.

———. *Unknown but Known*. New York: New American Library, 1968. Experiences with mystics and spiritualists are described to explain phenomena of communication with the "dead."

Godin, Andre. *Death and Presence*. Brussels: Lumen Vitae Press, 1972. Information is brought together, mostly from Europe, based on research into attitudes of life after death and the afterlife, with reports from outstanding researchers. Reflects the revolution in current thinking about death.

James, William. *Human Immortality*. New York: Folcroft, 1898. Rejects pantheistic view of immortality as survival in a "world soul." Pioneer of psychology suggests that mental life exists beyond death in an individualistic way.

Kutscher, A. H., ed. *Death and Bereavement*. Springfield, Ill.: Charles C. Thomas, 1969. Vivid descriptions of "beyond death" by persons who were reprieved from death. Documented case studies of actual experiences of persons who experienced death.

Lamont, Corliss. *The Illusion of Immortality*. New York: Ungar, 1965. Argues the belief that death is the end of human personality, and immortality is an illusion. Life is the only chance to achieve total personhood.

Lee, Jung Young. *Death and Beyond in the Eastern Perspective*. New York: Science Publications, 1974. Existential meaning of after-death states and reincarnation in classic Eastern philosophies.

Lepp, I. *Death and Its Mystery*. New York: Macmillan, 1968. Christian psychologist believes that immortality exists on the basis of meditation on universal evolution.

Lifton, Robert J., and Olson, Eric. *Living and Dying*. New York: Bantam, 1975. Authors present five categories of immortality: biological, creative, theological, natural, and experiential.

Moody, Raymond A., Jr. *Life after Life*. Covington, Ga.:
    Mockingbird Books, 1976. Physician interprets
    experiences of 50 persons who had undergone
    near-death situations, and draws some tentative
    conclusions about life after life.

Pike, James. *The Other Side*. Garden City, N.Y.: Doubleday,
    1969. Accounts of events preceding the premature
    death of Pike's son, and poltergeist occurrences after his
    death.

Stendahl, Krister, ed. *Immortality and Resurrection*. New York:
    Macmillan, 1965. Collections of essays on immortality
    and resurrection.

Unamuno, Miguel de. *The Tragic Sense of Life*. New York:
    Dover, 1921. Claims that man has "a hunger for
    immortality" and the total person exists beyond death.

Exercise Answers

1   The Face in the Mirror: Death and the Individual

1. F	3. T	5. F	7. d	9. d
2. T	4. T	6. T	8. c	10. d

2   Faces in the Crowd: Death and Culture

1. E	4. E	7. F	10. T	13. d
2. E	5. W	8. T	11. b	14. d
3. W	6. F	9. F	12. c	15. a

3   Stages on Death's Way

1. d	4. b	7. d	10. c	12. b
2. d	5. c	8. e	11. d	13. a
3. a	6. b	9. a		

4   Grief and the Dying Person

1. b	4. c	7. a	10. G	13. a
2. e	5. f	8. A	11. d	14. a
3. g	6. d	9. S	12. d	

5   The Final Wisdom: Learning from Death

1. T	3. T	5. b	7. d	9. a
2. F	4. T	6. b	8. d	10. a

6   Beyond Death

1. C	5. B	8. T	11. T	14. b
2. N	6. T	9. F	12. F	15. c
3. E	7. F	10. T	13. d	16. b
4. T				